Boy at the Commercial

Boy at the Commercial

Alick Rowe

With best wishes,
Alick Rowe

FABER AND FABER
London Boston

First published in 1978
by Faber and Faber Limited
3 Queen Square London WC1
Printed in Great Britain by
Latimer Trend & Company Ltd Plymouth

British Library Cataloguing in Publication Data

Rowe, Alick
  Boy at the Commercial.
  1. Hereford, Eng. Commercial Hotel   2. Hereford,
  Eng. – Social life and customs
  I. Title
  942.4´46   *DA690.H54*
  ISBN 0-571-10977-2

TO SIMON

℘ Contents

⅜ Preface

Writers are always being asked, at party, lecture or bar, where the ideas come from and did they always want to write. Usually they're idle, time-passing questions; everyone is interested in what makes other people do what they do, and firemen, dustmen, teachers and Grand Prix drivers must, presumably, face the same enquiry in one form or another. I'm usually bland in my answer: I was always interested in people, and always interested in reading and writing. There comes the time, however, when you have to ask the question of yourself.

A recent survey shows that men think of themselves as 'middle-aged' at 41·29 years; before that they're young. I want to know what it is that makes us middle-aged. It's not altogether physical: I feel much the same now as I did ten years ago. It may be something to do with seeing babies grow into children around us, and children into adults. It may be something to do with suddenly finding that what we used to consider habits are now constant. For me, it's very much to do with evaluations; at work, for instance, we find ourselves doing much the same sort of thing as we have for several years, with little prospect, particularly in these times, of beginning again differently, and yet as much as a quarter of a century stares us in the face before (at 64·9) we feel we're 'old'. So it becomes a period of assessing that future, and justifying, or exorcizing the past, of convincing ourselves, if we can, that the last signpost we followed has turned out to be the right one. 41·29 is a dangerous age and I'm running up to it fast. No coincidence, then, that writers in particular cope badly with this hurdle. Writing for a living is a lonely, demanding, precarious business. Most of us are pessimists and can be hell to live with in our self-contained world, drawing constantly on recollected emotions, distorted views of our own experiences, with the raw materials locked away in our heads and fearful of the time when the key may not turn, or we may find the mine worked out.

I was born at a good time and in a good place, just old enough to sense the uniqueness of the Second World War and too young to have to fight it. Hereford had the feel of an old town in another century until comparatively recently, and as the only child of a large, popular pub, I gathered, voraciously, that mixture of confidence and curiosity that a writer needs.

The stories, needless to say, have turned out differently from what I had expected. My original intentions were to write of Herefordshire and my large, unusual family, but when it came to it, I found I had written almost solely of life centred round the pub where I spent the greater part of my first eighteen years, and I was genuinely surprised to learn what it had meant to me. I was surprised, too, that I could not write with any intensity of my close family. It may be that they are still too near me and have not yet fallen into those clear patterns that intrigue in autobiography. Probably I shall have to wait until 64·9 for that.

The Commercial Hotel ceased to take guests shortly before the start of the war but still stands, new-minted as the Half Crown, opposite the bus station in Hereford, the last pub on the long walk down to the railway station. Commercial Road itself has changed a great deal. The 'skinyard'—an evil-smelling Victorian factory where the wool of sheep killed in the slaughterhouse a hundred yards away was scraped from the skins and baled—has given way to a filling station. The houses on the other side of the road have all come down, and Prail's Garage which adjoined them has moved to a more prosperous edge of the town, leaving a blank car park in its place, overlying the huge air-raid shelter that now presumably yawns dank and dark below. The Ritz, on the other side of the bus station, is now

an E.M.I. ABC; where queues waited for a night at the pictures
—sometimes diverted by a cartoon beamed to an outdoor
screen over their heads—the bingobashers now drift in and out;
the theatre organ that rose to play out the half-century in 1949
has long gone and the restaurant closed that used to send across
trays of Saturday lunch when the pub was too busy to waste
time cooking. The Grosvenor café and hotel is no more, and
Mrs. Twining's tidy shop and canteen, where I sang for ice-
cream or buns, is now blanked-out windows in a bricked-up
front, part of a factory. Commercial Road looks dead; no place
to be brought up now.

It was a paradise to me. I fire-watched with the men at the
skinyard for air raids that never came and was a popular
visitor in daytime, leaping from bale to huge woollen bale. My
beloved Cyril Squirrel was an almost daily casualty at the
ambulance station and sympathetically bandaged and patched
up. Mrs. Twining and the Colonel, who shared a delightful
cottage at the back of the canteen, were always glad to see me
and I was taken for any ride I wished by the drivers of the
G.W.R. horse-drawn drays as they passed the front steps. I
played avidly along 'the brook' which I never realized was
Hereford's disused canal, and among the derelict lorries and
in the timber yard of The Cut. I had a den in one of the many
abandoned air-raid shelters in the overgrown wilderness behind
the station itself. I was never warned off; people were always
kind to me, and I do not think they would have the time or
patience now.

I find the omniscience and total recall of autobiography
irritating because I know it is impossible. My childhood does
not yet fit together in one easy flow and these stories are simply
attempts at pinning down an experience. Everything in this
book happened and tells of a time just turning the corner behind us, out of sight. The stories are an honest attempt to answer
obliquely those two questions writers are always being asked.
If they don't answer them absolutely, they've given me some clues
and I don't think I shall ever be so bland in my replies again.

A. R.

₰ The Horse Man

Between the G.P.O. Sorting Office in the station yard and an aircraft-components factory, by the side of the long-disused canal, Frank Cotterel and his wife lived in a small brick house, Victorian redbrick, almost a cottage. Frank worked for the G.W.R.; he stabled the huge horses that drew the delivery drays round Hereford, and their rich dung provided for a large garden of most beautiful flowers and vegetables. He was the Horse Man and, to a child's eyes, was much like his charges: he was tall, slow, easy in his talk—you could never imagine the Horse Man angry, or in a hurry.

I knew the Cotterels for both horses and flowers. It was a Sunday morning task, much enjoyed, to run down Commercial Road to their neat, luxuriant estate, a half-crown in hand, to bring back whatever blooms it would buy for the lounge and Nan's room. The door to their house stood open throughout the summer and I would seldom have to tap: Mrs. Cotterel would see me running and come smiling to the door to take me into the garden, where together we would discuss what would best serve the purpose. She never forgot what flowers she had picked for me the previous week, and gravely we would wander along the bright rows to make our choice, a beautiful collection of blossoming colour growing tastefully in my hands. I liked best the time when the chrysanthemums, with their perfect shape, bronze shades and heavy scent, were in bloom. On special occasions, when I had maybe five or, rarely, ten shillings to spend, she would take greater care still, sending me home with an armful of her very best, and she would quietly draw from me details of the family's health and the nature of the celebration her flowers were to grace.

Before leaving, I was always taken to see the horses. Frank, on a Sunday morning, was invariably at work somewhere in the depths of his garden, acknowledging my arrival with a distant wave. But as his wife and I moved back towards the house, he would come to meet me, and while she took our selection inside to 'tidy up the flowers' and bind the stems with string, he walked with me to the dark stables where we would stand in silent admiration of the handsome beasts, patient during their day of rest. After this initial ceremony of silent worship, the Horse Man would quietly lead me to each gentle giant in turn, telling of some injury or strain one had suffered since I was there last, or of an unusual happening concerning another, and I would shyly stretch to stroke. We never visited them without some gift—apples, a bucket of feed, water—and after about ten minutes in their awesome company we would shut the lower doors and make our way to where Mrs. Cotterel stood holding the bunch of blooms, for which she accepted payment.

Even then I was aware that the Horse Man and his wife were anachronisms—their life a rural idyll set between the grime of the station and the shrill drilling and cutting of Aeroparts with its distinctive oily smell, and all less than five minutes' walk from the centre of the city. Whenever we passed their house, on the way to The Cut where a host of wrecked and abandoned lorries gave perfect freedom to long hours of imaginative play, one of them was always at work and would look up to wave from the rows of green and bright magic. And when I 'ran away' for the day—with full permission and, usually, a packet of sandwiches—and outside the Commercial hitched a trip round town on a dray, the adventure always ended at the stables. There I would be proud and happy to 'help' with grooming after the heavy harnesses had been taken from the animals—and Frank or his wife would be somewhere near, spade or fork in hand, to wave briefly before turning back to the rich earth. They were Kilvert figures, out of place in a

town, changeless and admirable in their quiet ways. Long before I left Hereford the horses had gone, of course, and when I
returned, after my years at university, it was to find The Cut
and canal cemented over and a second-hand car firm ensconced
in hideous concrete where I had left the Cotterels. I felt a shock
of loss, and still crane to try to catch a glimpse of where their
proud garden stood so splendidly as the Hereford train pulls
into the station; then I move through the clatter to collect my
car and drive through the changed world of my childhood,
aware of the gentle ghosts waving me by.

⚄ Christmas at the Commercial

It would all begin to happen many weeks before. The making of the puddings, of course, was the first sign that Christmas was not far round some sort of immediate corner, a reality, and the cake came next. But these were signposts of intent and the real excitement came sharply with the arrival of Ellsidon's Christmas catalogue. I've never known any book with the same ability to screw expectation six notches up in the pit of the stomach; here was Santa's plenty, if you could afford it—gifts, jokes, decorations. I liked the jokes best. There were the painless 'wifebeaters' of bright folded cardboard which made huge detonations when clapped across the ass of an aunt, indoor fireworks, black paper beetles to float on tea, hinged teaspoons to bend in the middle, soap that turned you black, mock soot, plates of thin metal that resembled broken glass when dropped. We all went through the catalogue—though none more keenly than I—seeking our different needs and diversions, and when the large impassive box was delivered by the postman, I knew for sure that Christmas was under way.

The decorations of previous years were brought out from Nan's boxroom and repairs were made, the irreparable replaced. I spent hours in the kitchen gumming coloured strips of paper into chains. The secret network of Christmas presents began— Bill slipped me cash for Mum's gift, Mum gave me money for Nan's and Bill's, and so on. The silver threepenny pieces were boiled sterile for the pudding and I sent my letter to Father Christmas lurching up the chimney on a column of smoke, knowing he didn't exist, and hadn't existed ever since Mum dropped my Christmas banjo down a whole flight of stairs, years ago on Christmas Eve, and was caught red-handed and giggling with her arms full of brightly wrapped boxes.

Only about a week to go, and the pub was transformed into a magic place of vivid papers, cotton wool, holly and strategically placed mistletoe. As ever, we would be fairly full this Christmas. It was Bill's big time: he threw open his house only once a year, he said, and his guests were welcome to everything he had. The amazing and beautiful fact was that he meant it. Bill was like that: no expense spared for his friends and his family, and when, at his death, people remarked how little he had left in the way of personal fortune, those of us who knew him well were in no way surprised and loved his memory the more.

With everything more or less prepared, there was nothing much to do but enjoy the few days before Christmas. The customers were a cheery lot anyway, but they became noisier and jollier as expectancy grew: I was allowed to release my Ellsidon's jokes on them. Carols began to be sung; more friends than usual were taken into our lounge for drinks; I gave a puppet show and floated about the place in a state of constant euphoria, dead drunk on adult bonhomie. Presents were wrapped and hidden tantalizingly, on top of wardrobes. At last it was Christmas Eve.

The tree came in from the conservatory to be new-rooted in a crisps tin disguised by crêpe paper with a layer of cotton-wool snow over sludgy earth from the back garden. The special tree decorations were brought out, and every addition of the well-known, well-loved spangles, tinsel, fairies, nutmegs, lanterns and fragile shining balls produced fresh wonder. Aunt Thelma had sent, from her new home in America, a record of her and her G.I. husband singing a song of their own, 'I'm Going to Hang My Balls on Your Christmas Tree, I've Got the Nicest Balls You Ever Did See', and we sang it as we festooned the branches. The star, less glittering and spiky than in earlier years, but impossible to replace, topped the highest branch, and finally the coloured lights were entwined and switched on. We all stood back to worship. We were not a religious family: we loved the time and its trappings, the fun, food, drink and each other.

For me, the final, tangible proof that it was all under way would be the arrival of Bill's brother, Uncle Rowland, with his wife, Tess, and my cousin, Carl, from Bishop's Castle. There they were at last, shouting greetings as they came through the bars. Carl was my own age, and as the grownups carried gifts, luggage, goose, cake in from the car at the door, we swapped footballing stories. And much later, after numerous visits to the uproarious bars, after carols on the steps from visiting singers with the whole house in deep, contented silence, after more jokes, more games, tipsy parents swept us unprotesting to our different rooms where we were eager to undress and get to bed, knowing we were only hours away from the greatest day of the year.

The night was short but the waiting long. At various times I would wake to find the room I shared with my mother, on special occasions of celebration or sickness, still empty, with only the hiss and pop of the gas fire to break the dark silence. Then came another wakening, when the warmth of my sleeping mother and the yielding, uneven weights on my probing feet told me everything was all right, and ready. And after that there was little sleep, if any. The delay as the clock crept round to a respectable seven o'clock was torture. The heaviness on my legs of a load of presents, just out of reach, wound me to fever pitch, and I lay in the warm dark, barely able to support the tension, hoping to communicate the urgency to the sleeping form at my side and waiting desperately for a grunt or the merest flicker of an eyelid—anything for an excuse: those long minutes would drive me crazy. Could I feign a coughing fit?

Then—*wham*. Mum stirred. I shouted 'Is it time?' and dived for the foot of the bed without waiting for an answer, landing on a beautiful jumble of sharp edges and crinkling paper. The light went on and . . . Oh God, oh God . . . just look. Mum kissed me happy Christmas, but first things first, and that meant the bulging sock on the brass bedstead—one of Bill's for greater capacity. Chocolate, an orange, a small book, sweets, a car, a diary, another car, more chocolate, toy soldiers, a miniature bottle of real port, sweet cigarettes, coloured pencils. Then the empty sock hit the floor and Mum was grinning up at me as she lit the gas fire.

A series of shouts and greetings from over the corridor and I'd beaten Carl by a long sock; we hurled greetings back but no time for triumph. Presents waited to be ripped into sight; the flat one first because it was Mum's and I knew it would be something to dress up in—last year it was a bus conductor's kit. This year . . . a thrashing of wrappings . . . and it was a cowboy outfit: hat, belt, guns, sheriff's star and spurs. I screamed my gratitude and tore into the rest as Mum ran through the litany of donors—that's from Nan and Bill; that one's from Thelma, Lloyd and Butch; Harry Jay's; that's another from me; that's from Les; Bill said you wanted one of those; I can't remember who that's from. There were games and books, a camera from Harry, comics, toys, a tiny cardboard bar counter stocked with tiny non-alcoholic drinks. The crumpled pile of wrapping paper grew at the side of the bed until the orgy was over and I sat, dumb at my good fortune.

The wireless was switched on: carols and bells. I remembered the bit about it being more blessed to give (though I didn't believe it), retrieved Mum's present from behind the chest of drawers and handed it over: a brooch. Then a last check on each tremendous thing and into my clothes. On with my kit too; there would be a sheriff at breakfast.

Tess made toast while Nan poured tea. It was a treat; we never bothered, usually. The day was over its first, best bit. Carl and I bore our armfuls down from the bedrooms into the Commercial Room where there was space to play. But the morning's fun would be in the bars and by midday we were there, to greet Harry and Doug, to cram mince pies into our mouths, to set up drinks for Phil. I rushed for my camera from Harry and used half the roll of film snapping tipsy customers and indulgent family.

By two the lounge was made ready for Christmas dinner. The best tablecloths stretched immaculately over the table, lengthened to its furthest extent and carrying a gleaming array of cutlery, cruets, glasses, plates. In the sweating kitchen, Nan was coping with the cooking on two gas cookers beneath limp paper chains. Puddings were boiling, the turkey roasting, gravy simmering, and trayloads of serving dishes standing ready as we all waited for the last customers to leave.

Some of them were to join us. Harry tapped at the kitchen door, bringing drinks for the cooks and news that the bars were almost empty. Les—next year to become my stepfather—could be heard carrying crates of empties down to the cellar. Jackie was with us this year, a likeable, lonely lady, with a limp and man's deep voice; she came pressing through to offer help, but it was all running to time. We would sit down about a dozen strong. Then Bill came in to stir everyone up; was nobody doing anything but him? A shocked melodramatic astonishment at the array of food and dishes. What was all this? He'd said bread and cheese this year!

Two courses, but massive, with champagne on the table for anyone who wanted it and glasses ready for varying tastes. Turkey, potatoes, sprouts, stuffing, gravy and bread sauce: plates went to and fro, filling, refilling; dishes were emptied and replenished. We were all hungry and Nan was a splendid cook. The pudding appeared, vast, dark, secret, and crammed with silver threepenny bits. Over it went half a bottle of brandy and out went the lights while Bill touched a match to the pool of spirit. We cheered the eerie blue flame. The lights went back on and Nan dished the pudding out, swamping it with sharp, sweet brandy sauce. Harry had a coin; a cheer. Another—Tess this time. Carl and I savaged our portions in frantic rummaging and—yes, but . . . a ten shilling note? I held it up, bemused, to more cheers and Bill's wink. Uncle Rowland demanded a coin and Nan said she'd seen one in his helping when she dished it out. Uncle Rowland's eyes boggled; he clutched his throat; we shrieked. He poured champagne down his throat and began to choke; we shrieked again. He coughed into his handkerchief and glared astonished, then smiled as he wonderingly held up the coin. It was a good act.

Mince pies for anyone? Well, maybe. Then, finally, toasts. Bill stood, solemn and sincere, raising his glass and wishing all beneath his roof a very happy Christmas—a moving moment for us all, sensing the strong bonds of family. Then the second toast: absent friends. This was quieter and there was silence as we recalled Uncle Cecil, brother to Bill and Rowland, who had died during the year, and Thelma, five thousand miles away in West Virginia, her first Christmas from home. Round the room eyes filled. Then Harry stood up shyly to thank Nan and Bill for their hospitality on behalf of the guests, and to wish us compliments of the season. We blinked away our emotion and forced back the party mood, slow but gathering: we had guests and would not involve them with private griefs. We staggered from the table. The second highlight of the day was over.

Now, although the routine of the day was attended to—the women tackled the enormous pile of washing up, there was Christmas cake and tea afterwards—things remained in a state of suspension until the bars were opened at seven and attention turned to the final miracle of Christmas Day, Bill's party in the Commercial Room.

In the pre-war days when the Commercial was a hotel, this had been the dining room; it had a speaking tube which ran down to the passage outside the kitchen. The floor was high-class rubber, a mysterious purchase from a liner at Southampton. It was a long room, and one wall was of glass sections interspersed with glass doors which led out on to a balcony overlooking Commercial Road. During one of Bill's wartime Christmas parties, while Brad Freeman and Mother were playing the piano, another G.I. had, for reasons best known to himself, climbed the front of the house and walked into the room through one of the glass doors, unluckily closed at the time; everyone said it was a most dramatic entry. Two-thirds of the way down the room, a heavy blue velvet curtain could be drawn across and this made a natural theatre for all sorts of festivities.

Nan, Mum, Tess and a band of helpers ran back and forth from the kitchen, setting the table in the room with cold turkey and other meats, bread and cheese, pickles, mince pies and cake. Les and Rowland, with other guests, began to haul crates of beer, whisky, gin and Guinness to one end of the room. A wide range of glasses stood ready. The Commercial Room, by ten, looked superb. Carl and I were no longer sent early to bed, our feeding bottles unfairly drugged with hot milk and gin, but were likely to be removed when we began to falter, or if the party became too boisterous. It usually lasted well into Boxing Day morning, till four or five, and it was not until we were teenagers that we managed to see it out, or share officially in the drinking.

The pub closes at ten but there is work for everybody, guests and all, before the party can take place. At last, when the house is ready for the morning, the rituals of the night begin. Bill insists, this year as every year, that all non-family must leave the premises as customers and return as friends, and solemnly everyone has been shown out and wished good-night, to wander a while along Commercial Road before turning back to be welcomed by Nan and Bill. They are urged upstairs, until thirty, maybe forty, of us are helping ourselves to drinks and singing carols, led by Mum at the piano.

The first hour is all singing and dancing; the popular songs of the time rise with the smoke and heat, quiet and contented. At midnight, the second ritual has to be run through. A large jug is filled with beer and we all move down to the steps of the Commercial to sing Christmas Day out. We fill the porch and spill on to the pavement, carolling, while smiling passers-by are wished good-night and fed with beer if they so wish. When Nan has had enough of the December air, she and most of the women file back upstairs but the men take their jug and songs a hundred yards down the road to the public lavatory on the corner by the station and give their performance all over again. From the porch or the balcony we hear the tipsy strains floating back and laugh at the lovely nonsense of it all, pointing out the amazement of people still in the streets and showing hilarious

anxiety at the occasional patrolling policeman, who will certainly be regaled with the jug when he meets the serenaders on
their return journey.

And after this, the party really takes off. The room grows
smokier, noisier, and carols give way to the favoured bawdy as
we get in a wide circle.

> *'We push the damper in, and we pull the damper out,*
> *But the smoke goes up the chimney just the same.'*

Actions go with the words and the splendidly pointless verse
loses one last word each time round, but all joining in the chorus:

> *'Stars of the evening . . .'*

(pointing them out)

> *'Shining on the shit-house door-oor-oor . . .'*

(and repeated)

> *'Stars of the evening,*
> *Shining on the shit-house door'*

(pointing wherever you imagine it to be or at anyone you particularly feel warrants the title. I get into a lot of trouble, this
way, but settle a few old scores). Then maybe 'Old King Cole',
again in the circle, with more specific gestures as His Majesty's
jugglers juggle with their balls in the air, or his painters slap it
up and down, or his plumbers advise him to stick it up his pipe,
up his pipe. Glorious: screaming it out in delight—two fingers
all round.

Now is the time for Phil to perform the One-Armed Conductor, which Uncle Rowland imported from the Buffs many
years earlier and bequeathed to the tall, angular Welshman.
Phil, on a beer crate, explains that he is the famous one-armed
conductor (and indeed his empty sleeve is tucked into a pocket
to prove it) who will now lead us, in deference to his native
land, in a rendition of 'Guide me, oh thou great Jehovah',
(except that we will all sing 'Beer from Edwardses, Beer from

Edwardses, feed me till I want no more' instead of the usual chorus). Piano please, and off we go until Phil stops us to apologize for his terrible cold but promises he will do his best, piano please, and off we go again, fervent in song and expectancy, but now . . . the famous one-armed conductor is about to sneeze. His eyes bulge, his nose twitches, he stops us to search for his handkerchief. But where to rest his baton? And behold—from the flies of his trousers a sly finger pokes out to curl round the stick as he sneezes mightily. A great scream rises, particularly from any newcomers, and Phil's bemused face peers at them, surprised at the fuss, while his good arm stuffs the hanky away and takes the baton from his protruding member, piano please, and off we go again, until the next sneeze, and the next. Jackie's face is a study. We cheer and cheer as the famous one-armed conductor steers us through the final Amen.

Somebody asks for the Palais Glide and the ranks form but have to wait while Mum demolishes one of the five gins and tonic on the piano lid; applause from us, a bow from her. The Palais Glide and it's fun and we're warmed up. The Hokey Kokey and the circle forms again. The dance begins but what Jack Parry is suggesting should be put in and out and shaken all about is definitely not feasible and gets a squeal from Phyllis, his wife. The surging chorus gets rough, and Tess, who has tactfully placed herself between her son and grand-nephew, works with Doug on the opposite side of the ring to make sure we don't get too battered. 'And that's what it's all about': Mother gives a final twiddle on the keyboard, the circle breaks up, hot and hungry, and Nan suggests we eat. During the eating, I tell Mum that I want to play the recorder and I'm allowed to run through 'Twelfth Street Rag' to her accompaniment. Everyone applauds, heartily kind, their hands full of sandwich, and I'm quietly warned off several encores but don't mind.

We're all doing justice to the spread but the party mood's strong and can't be contained; in any case, we've all eaten more today than we shall until next year and are more hungry for fun than food. Bill is not happy. I hear him complain, 'What's wrong with the buggers, Tess? They won't eat.' He roars above the hubbub, 'Drink, you buggers!' and we all cheer back, thought I see Tess slip from the room and wonder where she's going.

Time for a game. Uncle Rowland fixes a drawing of a donkey's rear end on the wall and produces a tassel and drawing pin for the blindfolded contestants to attach correctly to it. I know the game, of course, but secretly think it's a bit tame for the present company. I wait my turn on the other side of the curtains, and then I'm blindfolded, puzzled at the loud screams I've heard from previous players. The tassel is put in my hand and I move towards the wall. The crowd shouts 'No!' Uncle Rowland grabs my hand.

'Put your finger out!' and I do.

'It's here, boy!' and he plunges my finger into a surprise cold squidgy mess. I'm horrified and the room rings with screams and laughter as I jerk my hand back.

'Not up the donkey's bum!' shouts Rowland as I tear the blindfold off, laughing, to see him grinning as he brandishes an orange with a hole poked into the centre.

Carl's turn next and he's as surprised as I am. I'm hysterical with laughter—and so is Tess when she staggers in, dressed up as Grandma Buggins, to sing 'My Old Man Said Follow The Van'. She waves a wicker cage and we quieten down to hear the reason for her amusement. In the bottom of the cage is a torn-up mess of scraggly feathers and stuffing: our cat has been at the stuffed canary.

Carl and I run across the rubber floor to examine the remains as the room shares her laughter, then Mum strikes up the intro anyway and suddenly Aunty Tess is a cockney, strutting among us, singing and giving the cage a good shake now and then to see the feathers fly. She's marvellous and we tell her so as we shout and sheer and stamp. She promises Grandma Buggins at the Zoo later on. Phil is restrained with difficulty from leaving to catch a live pigeon in the bus station to cram in the cage as a replacement. Pity.

Nan wants Phyllis Parry to Charleston; she's a large lady but light on her feet. She's willing but somebody else suggests

'Sons of the Sea' and it meets with general approval. We form the circle. Mum strikes up the piano.

> *'Sons of the sea—bobbing up and down like this',*

and we bob up and down.

> *'Sailing the oceans—bobbing up and down like this',*

Harry is beaming and bobbing with difficulty.

> *'You may sail your ships, my lads—bobbing up and down like this'.*

Harry is bobbing up and down with even more difficulty.

> *'But you can't beat the boys of the bulldog breed—*
> *Bobbing up and down like this!'*

And inevitably, Harry is over on his backside, like Humpty Dumpty, and we go through it all again, faster. Other casualties: Jackie with her deep voice and limp concedes graceful defeat and Uncle Rowland helps her to her chair while we do it all over again, faster still. The room is full of cracking knees and breathless shouting. On the final bob, Horace lays hold of his neighbours, and his neighbours cling to their neighbours, turning the bobbing boys of the bulldog breed into a shrieking, giggling mass of struggling limbs on the floor.

Carl and I shriek for one more time but we're getting tired, over-excited, and looks pass between Nan, Mum and Tess, which we see, sensing somehow that time's running out for us. We retire quietly to the back of the room, hoping for reprieve.

Amazingly, Jackie hobbles to the piano. It's her first party here and we wait to see what she'll do. Mum nods and demolishes another gin and tonic as two more are added at the other end of the row on the lid; it's like putting fuel into a car. There's a surge of shhshhing as the piano ripples an introduction and the deep voice begins:

> *'I know an old lady who swallowed a fly.*
> *I don't know why she swallowed a fly . . .'*

She waves for us to join in the chorus but I don't know it and look wildly to see what's on other people's lips, fearful to be left out.

> *'Maybe she'll die.'*

And we hear the crazy story as that old lady swallows a goat to catch the dog that swallowed the cat which swallowed a spider that wriggled and jiggled and tickled inside her (horrible; I hate spiders) but she swallowed the spider to catch the fly and Jackie doesn't know why she swallowed the fly.

> *'Maybe . . . she'll . . . die'*

We're giving the chorus solemn strength now and splendid harmony as we slow it down. Then the old lady swallows the horse, and just as we're ready with our forty-part harmony, she dies.

> *'Of course!'*

Jackie shouts it out and we're caught. We cheer her; a really good effort.

Phyllis is no longer to be denied and steps into the middle of the room. Mum sees her and begins the Charleston which Phyllis deftly dances. Then we sit around to sing the old sentimental songs:

> *'If you were the only girl in the world*
> *And I was the only boy . . .'*

> *'If I had my way, dear, forever there'd be*
> *A Garden of Eden for you and for me . . .'*

> *'We'll meet again—don't know where—don't know when,*
> *But I know we'll meet again some sunny day . . .'*

And—horrifically—I yawn, almost asleep, before pulling myself together and hoping Mum didn't see. It's one-thirty and Carl and I are keeping a low profile, pushing our luck, but yes —damn—I do feel sleepy and friendly conspirators have been slipping me drinks all night.

B

Mum wants a rest from the keyboard and we give her an ovation as she manages to clear the lid of gin with a flourish. Rowland organizes games. An orange is passed along a row, between knees, and the process grows more and more grotesquely obscene as it progresses. The same teams pass a matchbox from nose to nose. Then Bill steps up for a quiet word with Rowland and they leave the room with a gleam in their eyes; good—something's going to happen. Tess runs a weird competition in which contestants sit on the sharp end of a quart beer bottle and place the heel of the right foot on the toes of the left while they open a matchbox and strike a match. It's a really ungainly sight and several seem to have done themselves permanent injury before Tess takes the bottle to perform the trick effortlessly; she must have been practising all year.

Mother seeks me out and says it's time I was going to bed but Harry rescues me. He's ready to sing his song. Mum returns to the piano and the room falls to silence; everybody likes Harry and knows what's going to happen. He stands by the piano and begins in a quiet vibrato:

> *'Climb upon my knee, sonny boy . . .'*

Warm, quiet smiles grow on everyone's lips. This is Harry's song and we wait for him to cry as he always does; Mum slides a grin at me to show there's no need to get as upset as Harry, but it's an oddly moving performance as the small tubby man stands awkwardly at the piano and the tears slide over his cheeks. Bill comes back into the room to make an announcement but sees that Harry is crying his song and waits respectfully at the door. He finishes and there's long, quiet applause. Harry wipes his eyes and moves to his seat as friends nod approval and smile congratulations.

Bill shouts that it's time for Tutankhamun, and his bedroom next door is too small to take more than a portion of the crowd that want to see. This is another adventure for those who do not know it. The room is dimly lit and, stretched beneath a sheet on Bill's and Nan's bed, is a still figure. Bill explains that this is Tutankhamun (we know it is Uncle Rowland) and novices are asked to demand of the oracle any questions they wish, as Tutankhamun knows all; but they must be quiet and respectful. Who's first? It just has to be Jackie and she's pressed forward into the dim circle of light and leans over the raised head to find the secret of the universe—when suddenly the other end of Tutankhamun rears up behind her, and arms grab her where no arms should be. Jackie has been addressing a pillow on Rowland's feet and she really seems to jump a foot in the air, with a squeal, as the room rings with laughter and the next novice is sent for.

Carl and I beg to be allowed to demand a question of the oracle, even though we've seen it before and know what will happen. But that is our fatal mistake and turns out to be our final fling. We're told to say good-night and stagger upstairs to a chorus of good will, bitterly protesting at the lack of the promised Grandma Buggins at the Zoo. But Tess whispers that she'll come up to give a special performance in Carl's room in five minutes and we creep upstairs, unwashed, washed out, to stagger into pyjamas.

As I pull on slippers to cross to Carl, I hear, from below, Phil singing his Jimmy Wilde song and can imagine the actions as he mimes a boxing match with the champion, ending on the floor as everyone joins in the last line,

> '*And let the rest of the world go by.*'

Then Tess is coming upstairs and I can hardly stay awake, even for Grandma Buggins; she can seldom have had a more somnolent, smaller audience. Carl is asleep almost before I leave blearily for Mum's bed, and as I drift back and forth on the edge of a tide of sleep, I hear, muted, from the Commercial Room, Bill singing on his knees to Nan:

> '*When you grow too old to dream*
> *I'll be there to remember*'

Then Nan and Mum, together:

> *Misty islands*
> *Of the Highlands . . .*'

At some stage I hear a strange voice which I just recognize as Les singing 'Ramona', and later the furniture in the room begins to shake and rattle as the party snakes all round the house in a conga, to shouts, whoops, giggles and frequent shhshhing from mothers with children of their own, remembering the two kids in their rooms at the top of the pub. There will be more songs, more dances and games before the men sing,

> '*Good-night ladies*',

growing slower and slower, more and more quiet, to emphasize the gallop of the chorus:

> '*Merrily we roll along, roll along, roll along,*
> *Merrily we roll along,*
> *O'er the deep blue sea.*'

But by then I'm away on a deep blue sea of my own, adrift in dreams, moving with steady regret from the enchanted isle, away from Christmas.

Not completely away, of course. Tomorrow—today—there will be the cribs to see in St. Peter's, All Saints, the Cathedral and the Catholic church. We shall walk to the Bull's Head to see Aunty Elsie and the girls—Cecil's family—and in the afternoon there will be the match at Edgar Street. For lunch there will be goose from Bishop's Castle, and I shall wake late to find Tess at one end of the Commercial Room, with Mum at the other, buckets in hand, scrubbing out the footmarks from the rubber floor, while Nan stands dazed at the door, wondering how they can face it.

In a day or two, Tess, Rowland and Carl will have to go back to B.C. It's a sad thought, but the New Year's party in the lounge will be a worthy echo of last night's glory. At some time in the coming year I shall be given Dickens's *A Christmas Carol* to read, and, closing the book after reading of the wild Christmas party he creates, I shall not be too impressed. He should have been with us last year.

⅜ Kruger's Independence

One of the more fascinating aspects of my childhood was the realization that my family all had split personalities, were as false as hell; pub life contained such opposites that hypocrisy became as much part of the tools of the trade as clean hands and well-polished tables. To treat, for example, a surly customer from the unpredictable Public Bar to the same welcoming smile as a personal friend from the Private; not to scream, for example, at the habitual jokes of the habitual bores but to laugh heartily and risk another dozen. The two faces became welded inseparably into one amiable mask. My grandfather, Bill, was master of this art.

Another contrast was between public boisterousness and private gentility. You needed to escape occasionally from the almost constant good humour of the bars, and the main retreat was the upstairs lounge, richly carpeted, with a radiogram, deep armchairs, an ancestral sideboard with lions rampant as legs and, yes—even a baby grand piano. The upstairs lounge had much else too; it was a sanctum of the genteel. I came to use it a lot—especially when the need for serious music swept into my life. But at the time I'm writing about it was the equivalent of the standard front parlour, holy with unuse.

This contrast, this day-to-day mixing of working-class bawdy with middle-class pretensions, frequently cut the ground from beneath my innocent feet in the years before I began to appreciate the rules of the game. At the Baptist chapel Sunday school, which I used to attend, incongruously, through the honourable connection with my Scout troop, I more than once responded to the hearty call for a hearty song with a hearty rendition of some pub number of whose gross *double-entendre* I was simply ignorant. When my primary school teacher asked if any child had a good story to tell the class, boy, I had a hundred! I didn't actually understand any of them, but I knew our customers laughed when they heard them, and that they thought them even funnier when I delivered the goods; they would roll about.

Perhaps it was the realization of this dilemma—no dilemma to me—that prodded Mother and Nan to do the genteel thing and invite my first teachers to tea. This was an upstairs lounge occasion, with all the stops pulled out, to persuade my mentors that pub life was not all booze and bawdy, as they may have gathered from me, or that whoever's fault it was that they were teaching a six-year-old degenerate it wasn't Mother's or Nan's. Miss King came with Miss Jones: spinster ladies both. Miss King had a moustache, and I was very fond of them both.

The tea party was to begin immediately after school, and Miss King and Miss Jones walked home with me. It strikes me now that they may well have been as intrigued at the prospect of visiting the pub as I was proud at having them. Anyway, we walked the half-mile or so from All Saints to the Commercial, cutting through the Burial Ground where I probably showed them the crumbling gap in an ornate Victorian tomb into which we kids dared each other to go—though none moved far into that ghost-ridden black.

Miss King and Miss Jones would have come to the front door and, I imagine, been fascinated as they went along the narrow passage separating the two bars, still heavy with smoke and smell from a busy lunchtime. They would have been fairly hurried upstairs past the downstairs lounge, another sanctum but well used, for, under the invariable rule that he was not to be disturbed before tea, Bill would be stretched out snoring by the fire. Bill, you see, this day as many days, had enjoyed a heavy lunchtime both sides of the counter; Bill was sleeping it off and would be safe down below until family tea-time—by which time Miss King and Miss Jones would have departed, hopefully in warm surprise that we could be as civilized as the next family.

Upstairs, the superior gas fire was lit and the heavy curtains drawn to keep out partly the dusk and partly the sight and sound of the tanning factory that spread on two sides. While Nan brought the tea, Mother played the piano—real music, popular classics, not the wartime songs we had been bawling in the downstairs lounge at the week-end when the G.I.s from Bradbury Lines had been over with Ivory soap and Manhattan cookies. I sat politely at Mum's feet, warned to be A Nice Boy and Nan arrived, smiling, with a tray of buttered toast, tea, cakes. It was very civilized, and if Nan and Mum were talking in a funny way—rather slower, higher, with no cursing at all—well, fine: I was already old enough not to be surprised at anything that happened at home. Would we have a knees-up? Probably not: maybe Miss King and Miss Jones had no knees. The grownups talked about the war, All Saints, my progress, Hereford; the gas fire popped and hissed. It was very cosy with smiles all round above the best tea set. I was quietly dozing, bored. It was very nice. Nan and Mum must have thought they were winning.

They had reckoned without my glorious granddad Bill. Waking alone downstairs, the unravelled sleeve of sleep and sobriety not even half knit up, he had wondered at the piano music floating down to him through the ceiling. Remembering, then, the visit of Miss King and Miss Jones, and the necessity for making it a success for my sake, Bill had listened carefully for laughter, maybe even applause, but had—long after the music had died away—heard nothing at all. To all of us, silence meant failure, boredom. When people enjoyed themselves they shouted, cheered, rattled their glasses, stamped, danced, clapped, wept; they did not sit in silence. Bill sprawled in the darkness, wondering how to do his bit.

The walls of the Public Bar were mostly bare: there was a large painted mirror over the fireplace proclaiming the merits of Black and White whisky, but that was about all. In contrast, the Private Bar had two mirrors, a pastoral print, a framed set of photographs showing the key figures in a local murder trial of long ago, and it had 'Kruger's Independence'.

'Kruger's Independence' was a political cartoon. It showed the Boer leader in a long nightgown complaining to John Bull, 'You have taken away everything. All I have left is my independence.' The problem was posed at the bottom of the cartoon: 'Puzzle: find Kruger's independence.'

It had been a mystery to me all my life. I never expected to understand it but I would have liked at least to know the area in which its humour lay. For it was certainly funny; I knew that. It was dated 1904, forty years earlier, but it still made men laugh—and women even more than men; it made them laugh suddenly, the way they laughed at the punch-lines of my dirty jokes. One moment they would be blank and puzzled, reading the cartoon on the wall, scanning it, then Bill would hand it down to them for closer examination. They would peer closely at it, this way and that, moving into the light at the windows to see it better, and then they would laugh—laugh that particular laugh that you never heard on the radio. I accepted it simply as part of adult life, like enjoying beer and driving a car. One day I would understand but until then—in spite of longing—'Kruger's Independence' would have to remain a mystery. I had no idea who Kruger was: he sounded foreign, nasty.

So when Bill burst into the upstairs lounge waving 'Kruger's Independence' and beaming happily, I snapped at once from my bored reverie. Mum and Nan were surprised too. Miss King and Miss Jones broke off their chatting to smile at him in polite enquiry as he brandished the picture before them. Bill said nothing, but he seldom talked unless he had to. For a moment, nobody moved and nobody spoke. I was delighted; I knew the Misses would like the picture—everyone did. Trust Bill to know how to get the party going; we would have knees-up any moment, and then the bottles would arrive.

Incredibly, Nan and Mum were not delighted. Nan's face

could screw up into a formidable weapon when necessary. We seldom suffered, but when a customer was just too rude, too demanding, too much a nuisance, Nan's face usually stopped him in his tracks. It hit Bill so hard now that it penetrated even his heavy armour of boozy *bonhomie*. He gaped, recoiled towards the door. As the Misses strained to keep polite curiosity in their eyebrows—Who *was* this? Did he want them to look at that picture?—Bill seemed to shrink. He dithered, nodded solemnly and retreated, clasping 'Kruger's Independence' to his chest like a bandage. I looked on brightly. What next?

What next was Mum moving quickly back to the piano, and Nan gathering the tea things on the tray. From the exchange of glances as one pressed the keys and the other opened the door, something had happened. Nan's face said someone was in for it; Mum's said someone had been A Bad Boy. And then, magically, in the split second before Ivor Novello and the closing of the door, they grinned at each other. I grinned too, and spluttered, happy with them for yet another good joke I never came within spitting distance of. But Mum said sternly, 'Sshh', and I did, aware of not being A Good Boy. I slipped a sly glance at Miss King and Miss Jones, to see if they'd noticed, but they were all polite enjoyment again: one nodding to the music and the other wiping crumbs from her moustache. They were having quite a nice time, from the looks, but I was sorry it was all so dull for them—no dancing, no Americans, no cookies, no soap.

So the tea party came to an end, and if we ever repeated the experiment, I have no recollection of it. I don't know what benefits anyone got as a result; I remember no changes at All Saints. Miss King and Miss Jones continued to treat me as they treated children who had not taken them home to tea, which seemed a bit unfair.

I do know that Bill stumbled down to the lounge, and then, in terror at the pursuing Nan, must have fled, because when I went in some hours later while everybody was working in the bars, 'Kruger's Independence' was lying neglected, face down on a chair. I picked it up, peered at it, turned it round and round, read the words for the hundredth time and still made no sense of them. I took it to the lamp to see better.

And behold! As the lamplight fell briefly on the back of the picture, all was very definitely revealed and I saw why everyone laughed. You didn't have to understand about Kruger, or anything. Kruger's body was silhouetted beneath his nightgown, which turned transparent when light struck through the back. I just couldn't believe it. Snaking heavily down almost to the hem of his gown, from the base of a very round tummy, was a massively proportioned penis. Boy, it was the biggest dickydido I'd ever seen in my life! It was enormous. Speechless with delight I bore the picture round the room, holding it up to the light bulb, to the standard lamp, to the light through the window above the door. And still that vast appendage swung down to Kruger's feet.

I was dazed with the joy of discovery. If I didn't know who Kruger was, I certainly knew all about his independence! I laid the frame reverently back on the chair and ran upstairs, hugging myself. I couldn't wait till the morning—just couldn't wait to tell Miss Jones and Miss King what they'd missed.

৪ Detective

Detective was by far the most brilliant man I ever knew and I was privileged to be his companion and assistant for two or three years of early childhood. He wasn't posh like Lord Peter Wimsey or weird like Sherlock Holmes, and he wasn't much to look at. In fact, he was quite small, with light brown hair and eyes like mine, but his courage was as ten men when roused and he was magnificent in his fury. I never let him down during our years together, no matter what odds were ranged against us; we fought evil at all levels.

Often he was seconded to the British Forces fighting in Europe, who were glad to have him there, for many were the terrible enemies he destroyed. His cunning was immense, and like all good sleuths he was a master of disguise. When the enemy ambushed a whole company of Americans, including soldiers we knew personally from Bradbury Lines, and used the captured uniforms and vehicles to lure further unsuspecting allies into ambush, only he could have formulated the brilliant plan of waylaying a German general and turning the trick against the foe by dressing himself in the officer's uniform and leading the fake company into disaster. We were decorated by George VI for that, for he had wanted me as his driver during the ruse, tutoring me in a few German phrases—he being of course multilingual. When we released our American friends, their gratitude was overwhelming: they had never expected to see the Commercial again, and pressed gifts on me, including a storm trooper's belt and dagger, which I have to this day.

I think that was our greatest triumph, but the truly wonderful part of our relationship was that Detective somehow found time to help me out in my petty troubles at school and home. At times of despair I needed only to send out the secret signal to bring him to my side, unseen—for he was well skilled in all forms of concealment.

The day, for instance, that Miss Caldicott made me cry, he was there within minutes, watching the school through binoculars from high on the roof of the electricity works next door. We talked the matter over on the way home, and that night he brought her cringing to my room and forced her to her knees to beg my forgiveness and confess amid copious tears, her own this time, that I had been wrongly accused; it was Roger Speake, not I, who had done it.

And when, on my way to All Saints, I saw a lorry bearing a wrecked fighter plane along Widemarsh Street, closely followed by a smaller vehicle piled high with wet, glistening skins, suddenly Detective was at my side without even waiting for the signal, an arm round my shoulder, comforting my distress: yes, I was right—those slimy skins were all that remained of the brave crew from the crashed plane, but we would have our revenge. And we did. We were in France that very night, overhearing a drunk officer of the Luftwaffe boasting of the plane he had shot down over All Saints while Detective brushed luminous paint on the wheels of his jeep so we could follow the gleaming blobs to the enemy airfield and spray vengeful bullets into the pilots as they rushed out to their planes in answer to the fake alert he had arranged.

Sometimes there was no crime to be avenged, no wrong to be put right, and he would come to me in quiet moments of numb loneliness to chat over the state of things; we would talk of United's last game, or of Stone Farm, where he had so often saved me from the charges of wild bulls, high-spirited horses and mad dogs. Sometimes even there was nothing to be said and he would watch, smiling, from the corner of the room, offering company and reassurance, always knowing what my needs were. He once saved the penalty that gave my beloved

Tottenham Hotspur victory over the detested Chelsea. Detective was the best friend I ever had.

Detective managed to stay concealed from my family, though there was a near miss once. We held a midnight service in memory of a school friend who had been killed in a road accident that afternoon. The service was definitely High Church, with candles on a tray to catch the wax, and my wooden crucifix with a leaden, worn Jesus. We were well into the hymn 'Now the Day Is Over' when, to our shock, we heard Mum and Les outside the door, raising a joking counterpoint to our devotions —'Good King Wenceslas', if I remember rightly. We were mortified at their mocking and had the candles out in seconds, and Jesus stuffed underneath the pillow, but I think this event heralded the break-up of our time together, for it was about this time that Detective's visits grew less frequent. Maybe he saw I had a new stepfather and thought the Commercial simply wasn't big enough for the two of them. But he stayed my secret companion for a while until, as I made more friends at St. Owen's, his visits ceased altogether. Somewhere during my time at the new school he must have retired altogether and I sincerely hope some other small child benefited from his special attentions and never-failing loyalty.

This is the first time I have ever betrayed the secret of his existence. He was altogether in a different, more real and vital class from the two angels who, in earlier years, had sat either side of my bed, glimmering palely to lull me to sleep, confident of their watchfulness against the spiders. And also from the strange presence, never seen by me but very real in the darkness, who gave me the power to raise the foot of my bed from the floor and let it bang down at will, causing Mum to call out from the next room to ask what the hell I was doing. I never told her about him, either, and I don't much like to think about him now.

♫ Harry Jay

I read a letter in a national newspaper a while ago complaining bitterly of the vestigial remains of our class system: the writer, among other examples, mentioned first and second-class railway carriages but not, strangely, the Public and Private bars of the majority of our pubs. Certainly it was the difference between the bars of the Commercial that helped me eventually to identify Them and Us. The Commercial was not a plush or a posh pub: the greatest of our customers were—like ourselves, I suppose—lower middle class, and these used the Private Bar where they paid an extra penny on most drinks for the privilege of a slightly higher standard of décor, being served for the most part by one of the family and not having to mix with the generally working-class clientele of the Public. Much of my early life was spent in the Private Bar. The rougher, noisier customers boozed next door and I felt always uneasy having to collect there for charity or to take in messages. Members of the Public Bar seemed to me intruders or, at the best, unlooked-for visitors, whereas the regulars of the Private were virtually family. Of these, the closest to me were Harry Jay and Phil Davies.

Harry and Phil were another contrast, even in shape: Phil was long and thin: Harry was short and distinctly tubby. Then again, Phil was Welsh and Harry a Herefordian. Phil was the active man: he had a family, had served in the war as a drum major in the Middle East; his main party piece was the bawdy imitation he gave every Christmas of a one-armed conductor finding an unusual part of the body with which to hold his baton when he needed to blow his nose. He became a long-distance lorry driver and took me on my first visit to London; when I was stood on the Private Bar counter to sing for pennies, Phil took round the hat for me.

Harry was a bachelor, passive and shy, a quiet onlooker, who had been a foreman carpenter and painter with the same firm almost all his life. Things tended to happen and leave Harry on the outside. Even when he was appointed captain of the Drifters—a crazy darts team, playing purely for fun—it is Phil I remember, with his massive wooden darts case holding three tiny darts, or Doug Phillips with his manic cackle of laughter balancing on a beer crate to pitch the dart. Only once do I remember the Harry of these days involved in a drama, and his reaction was typical.

Unbelievably, Harry was beaten up one night on his way home from the Commercial. Collecting his bicycle from the dark alley at the back of the pub, he was attacked and suffered bruised and cracked ribs, though I never knew why, and for the mild Harry to provoke such a response still seems amazingly unlikely. Another of our regular customers was strongly rumoured to have arranged the attack, and I happened to be with Harry near the coke fire in the Private Bar when this adversary pushed through the crowd to order his drink from a place directly opposite. The bar fell silent, and for a while the men studiously ignored each other. But the temptation of the aggressor both to demonstrate and to disclaim responsibility grew too great, and he stared pointedly at Harry over his pint, until Harry was forced to meet his eyes.

In the silence, the adversary said, 'Hello, Harry.'

Harry slowly dropped his gaze to the half-pint before him and muttered, without looking up, 'Hello, Horace.'

And that was that. I stood at Harry's side and my eleven-year-old heart lurched and thundered at his mild patience and humiliation.

I loved both Harry and Phil dearly, but of the two I suppose Harry's shape and shyness were the more appealing to a small child, and I was devoted to him from as early an age as I can remember; he was part teddy bear, part Pickwick—the perfect adoptee uncle. And maybe even more, for I barely had a father until Mother remarried when I was ten. It comes as a shock to realize that I recall Harry in such clear and varied terms, whereas my grandfather, Bill, has retreated to a part of my memory from which I can only conjure admiration, awe and pride. Bill was a god to me, successful, important, even intimidating; Harry was never like that.

Harry, then, was much nearer family than customer, and his whole life must have revolved round the pub where he was a nightly visitor, and at lunchtimes too at week-ends. He played crib for the pub team, darts and that odd-sounding game phat. He was never late for the regular pub outings and would be ready at the coach, waiting red-faced in his dark blue suit with its bulging waistcoat, his grey limp mac over his arm. On birthdays, anniversaries, triumphs, weddings, at the annual gargantuanism of Christmas and New Year's, there would be Harry, quiet in a corner, beaming at the company, sipping the whisky he could be pressed to take for colds or on special occasions, simmering in deep content, singing very quietly when we all were bawling our heads off, giggling at the outrageous songs, dances, games and party pieces. On such occasions he called my grandparents Bill and Win, but he had a nice appreciation of formality and would revert to Mr. and Mrs. Edwards when respect was called for. Every one of the large crew of relations knew, liked and respected Harry, expecting to see him near the coke fire whenever they came, drawing him naturally into the conversation and nodding for him, and one or two other close friends, to retire with us to the downstairs lounge when a family booze-up seemed in the offing. Of course, what I didn't realize then was that we were as much family to him as he was to us. He came frequently to our Christmas dinner table and a room would be made ready to save him the long, lonely cycle ride from one end of Hereford to the other, or for him to rest in when he felt like peace and quiet. Harry had trouble with his feet and a unique gait which became more pronounced as he tired: then his limp became almost a waddle. The devotion I felt for him was quite mutual.

Until grammar school began to draw me out of this wild, secure existence, at twelve or so, I lived a rich and privileged life. I was spoiled to death—the only son of a pretty and popular young mother in the pub of successful, respected grandparents. I sang for money, played the recorder, played the piano, played darts for absent Drifters, performed puppetry, even served drinks and generally foisted myself on people's goodwill and patience whenever I could. Ridiculously, I can never recall being put down for my precocity, which I know I often deserved. And there always was Harry: seldom enthusing over any of my ventures—he was a man of few words—but approving, encouraging with a nod.

I must have reached a stage where I needed that nod as a seal of approval. Nan brought him in to hear my swoony efforts at Debussy's '*Clair de Lune*'; he watched solemnly my attempts at fretwork and ordered a calendar for Christmas; when I produced *The Commercial Times*—a weekly tabloid of twelve faint copies—Harry was the first to come to the kitchen to buy a copy. He took me to football matches; he gave me a Meccano set and a camera, two of my most prized possessions. I had money for a treat every birthday, with a card, and I always had to seek him out by the fire to tell him how the party had gone. I was a sickly child and often in bed. Harry was always a regular visitor, never staying long or saying much, but totally necessary to me. From early childhood into my teens, his presence was more important than his words; his visits became ritual, and you can award no greater accolade than that.

If I ever let Harry down at these times I've conveniently forgotten the shame. I don't (equally conveniently) count my fumbling attempts at woodwork, for I simply had no aptitude. When the lessons began at my secondary school, Harry advised on my white, pouched carpenter's apron, and while I struggled to get a mortise and tenon joint to fit, which it never did, he showered tools of all sorts on me and slipped me wood from his

firm every now and then. But all to no avail: my measurements
were never exact or my saw cuts straight. The only thing that
ever turned out as it should was a long thin rod, worked pains-
takingly on the lathe, which Mr. Worthing beat me with for
talking—and then it broke. I turned my ambitions towards the
Church, one change of direction from a partial vocation as a
teacher.

Bill died in 1952, when I was fourteen, and the end of my
childhood saw too the slow decline of life as it had been at the
Commercial. Nan took over the licence and Mother was still
there, with Les, my stepfather; Thelma, my aunt, Bob and
Butch were still there. The staff were mostly long-standing
friends; there were still parties, triumphs, fun, but bit by bit the
permanence evaporated. My parents took a pub of their own
and eventually I lived at the Commercial only during the week
and spent week-ends at the Kite's Nest before moving there
permanently. School became a way of life and I seemed to see
Harry and Phil less, though I know they remained quietly
proud of my successes there. Thelma took Butch to America,
and Bob found his way to Canada. It was all changing. When I
called in at the Commercial on occasional visits, it was still a
haven of sorts, though the clientele was changing too; Nan,
Harry and Phil were still anchors. Then Nan left and retired
to a bungalow near the Kite's Nest. The Commercial moved
into family legend.

One desperate memory occasionally comes back, even now,
in bad dreams. The final Christmas of Nan's tenancy, we all
made a great effort to recapture the flavour of the past and for
once came near succeeding. The house was full and the party
ran until four or five in the morning. I was master of ceremonies
and did my best to stand in for Bill. It was a wonderful night,
still talked about when the family gets together, which I regret
for the sharp, cruel comparison with the Christmas night that
succeeded it. In the tiny, cluttered sitting room of Nan's new
bungalow, a few of us, survivors, gathered to see out Christmas
Day, but never were ghosts more apparent: my parents were
exhausted after a hard week at the Kite, and a handful of

friends toiled to create something that might blot out the harsh comparisons. No good. Eventually we fell into silences that really were too deep for tears. Harry sat in the corner, his eyes on his glass, for once the contentment gone; no giggling. There was no piano to cheer us; no space to move. There was drink and Nan did her best, but, one by one, as in a Chekhov play, the guests departed and the sadness spread like a soft grey cloud.

But Harry still cycled nobly for four miles to the Kite each Sunday unless wet. Mother would come to find me if I were at home. 'Harry Jay's here.' And I'd leave school work or the Sunday papers to join him in the bar; no Phil with him now, and no coke fire, no chair of his own. And, horrifically, I was changing too—often reluctant to leave work going well or the papers, to spend half an hour with this old friend, much of it in silence. Things in common were harder to come by.

Then I left Hereford for five years, teaching and working for a university degree. I returned, in 1963, a boarding house tutor at the school I'd so much loved as a boy.

More changes. Phil was dead, and lesser-loved figures had aged or followed him. Nan was suffering with severe arthritis, though incredibly it was T.B. that was to kill her within a year or two. But amazingly Harry was not only working and working well, but working at the school. In the yard an ugly, cheap modern block was rising, decorated by his firm. I couldn't have been more pleased, and invited him to a cup of tea in my study the first morning break I could; it was a disaster.

The intervening years had spun some separation between us that neither could identify or push aside. He wouldn't sit down and soil my chair with his overalls. He stood instead at the opposite end of the room, ill at ease, sipping his tea as fast as he could. There was nothing to say. Boys came knocking for permission to do this or that, staring at the strange dumpy figure in grubby white overalls in the corner of my study. Something demanded my absence for a minute or two and when I returned Harry was still there, leaning against my bookcase, though his empty cup had been placed alongside my own. As the sense of loss sharpened, I heard myself mouthing smug and superior inanities about Cambridge, about the Cathedral School, as Harry listened in polite solemnity. It was the hardest of the many realizations that I had been drawn out of my beginnings and left loose in a limbo from which, in more than one sense, I've never found a way. It was painful. We talked about my parents, Phil, the good old days, but it was all small talk and I was glad when eventually the bell rang and he could go.

The visit to my study upset me so much that I set work for my class and went to find him again. I wanted to say something to him that at least showed warmth and gratitude, but when I came upon him, painting in the new block, there were people about and a class the other side of the door, and to call him away to my study or the yard would be frighteningly magisterial. I watched him, unseen: a much-loved figure, uncomfortable on his knees, engrossed in the craft of brush-strokes, and I went back to my class, unable to lose myself in such skills.

As the new block neared completion, of course I saw Harry often. There were waves and smiles in passing, but nothing more; I never tried to talk to him at length again as the school year and the firm's contract ran out side by side. The boys used to tell me of the small, fat painter who would shyly chat, and how he would proudly say that he'd known me for years. And when I returned to Hereford, at the end of the holidays, Harry Jay was dead.

'Harry Jay's dead. Isn't it a pity?'

Mother told me the facts. Harry had, for the only time in his life, constructed a drama round himself by taking his own life. He had cycled home after work, locked the door and changed into pyjamas, stuffing his soiled clothes into a sack. He had written letters, pinned a note to the door, locked it and finally laid his head in the gas oven. There was something pitifully typical about his careful details and the note which told whoever should come looking for him to fetch help and not try to get in. Harry never wanted to hurt or be a nuisance to anyone.

'Harry Jay's dead.'

Various friends had different explanations for his action,

though, when I told my headmaster how saddened I was, I heard another: 'Silly Mr. Jay thought he had cancer'. We sat at coffee after dinner, the first night of term, in the drawing room of his Georgian house. 'Poor silly Mr. Jay.'

One of the workmen had died. Poor silly Harry Jay. It hit me hard. Harry and the *Commercial Times*; Harry at our table; Harry at football matches; Harry playing darts, at my mother's and step-father's wedding. The whole of Harry Jay's involvement with me closed round. Riding to my great-aunt's pub on Harry's crossbar; Harry in my sickroom; Harry silent with me after Bill's funeral. The long, lonely cycle rides, the shy giggle. There must be a better epitaph.

I tried to explain, to talk of these things and the headmaster and his wife listened politely, but as I talked my eyes wandered round his room, over the good prints, the long flow of curtains, the antique mirror, the grand piano; they took in the total good taste, the middle-class elegance to which he had always been accustomed. There was no way this man could understand the loneliness of the only child and the bonds that had been tied with the ageing, shy bachelor. No way he could appreciate the chaotic boozy parties in the smoke-filled rooms of the Commercial I thought of the mad Drifters and the crazy games, the dirty jokes, the bawdy songs. What could it mean to the headmaster of a public school? Harry and Phil, bearing me in turns on their bikes to the Bull's Head through the derelict station yard, had once, laughingly, wiped my infant backside with dock leaves when I'd been taken short. The polite faces smiled on with a show of understanding but not understanding, and I stopped.

I have never let myself think intensively of Harry and his part in my life until now. Much happened in the dozen years since my rambling monologue in that Georgian drawing room— including the irony that, even as my headmaster was telling me of poor silly Mr. Jay who thought he had cancer, a cancer was building in him which would lead to his own death some four years later. It has been for me a time of change and gaining perspective. What worries me now about Harry is the slow deterioration of joy in his life. Harry, happy as part of us at the Commercial; Harry, desolate in Nan's bungalow that terrible Christmas night. Harry, beaming at his Drifters; Harry, with no place at the Kite's Nest. Harry, giggling at my ecstasy as United scored a goal; Harry, in the far corner of my study, sipping tea and wishing himself elsewhere. Harry, above all (and the more vividly, as I was not there), loading his clothes into a paper sack and laying his face on an oven grill. I know I have had a part to play in such a man's death.

I am not much moved by death. Some mechanism far inside me seems to prohibit mourning. I loved Nan and Bill but could not grieve for them: it is a very real deficiency. But ridiculously I feel, now, at this moment, the loss of Harry Jay as a misery which I fear will deepen, and much of what I do for the rest of my life will be trying to say something to myself that I could not say to my headmaster, snug in his well-bred gentility, or to Harry himself that morning in a school corridor as laboriously, red face furrowed in concentration, he painted a door white.

⸙ The Chinese Burn

Writers are always being asked where the ideas come from, and when did they first begin writing stories. Looking back from this distance a string of random events shakes itself into some sort of order and a number of happenings, usually small, begin to point the way to an answer to the second, even if the first question remains defiantly unanswerable. Looking back, I think I've been dramatizing all my life.

There is, for instance, the time when I truly believed I was going to die. My first real pen was hollow, and sitting in proud and messy thought with my first pen in my first bottle of ink, I sucked in deep meditation, somehow managing to forget that one end of the pen was in the ink and the other in my mouth. My eight-year-old self downed a good quarter of permanent blue-black and knew I had poisoned myself. What pride or stupidity stopped me mentioning the fact to any of the adults at home, I don't know, but I tottered up to bath and bed where I composed my first remembered verse—presumably in pencil:

> *If I die tonight as I think.*
> *Just by swallowing ink.*

I placed the first fruits of creation reverently beneath my pillow for posterity and must have felt pretty stupid in the morning when I woke, not to Jesus and glorious resurrection, but in the dingy back room near the bathroom.

But anything for drama. I feel even more stupid when I recall what I did to Mrs. Hunt.

Roger Hunt was one of my school friends at St. Owen's Secondary. He lived behind a shop in Commercial Street, not far from the Commercial. We were both friendly with the Stones who lived above a garage midway between, and for a while we spent a lot of time together: me, Roger, Michael and their respective sisters Liz and Janet. The girls were older than us, but not much. We boys were all about eleven and in the same class.

We did not call ourselves a gang, but there were others in the area who did. There was the gang who had the district behind the railway station; they were rough and used to harass a gang of my own. Another gang patrolled the streets near the Stones' garage, particularly the disused graveyard called quaintly the Burial Ground. This gang were, strictly, of no concern to me as I was not in their territory, but finding myself in the loose federation of Hunts and Stones, I had to accept that their enemies were mine. The alarming difference between this last gang and the rest was that the toughest members were a couple of girls whom I remember as much older than any of us—though in all truth they were much the same age as Liz and Janet.

One day these Amazonettes led their gang to pursue us and cornered the girls in the Burial Ground, leaving us boys as small fry, not worth the effort. There was no question of an heroic rescue: we knew when we were well off and watched huge-eyed from a good distance as Liz and Janet were tortured with the dreaded Chinese Burn and made to cry. The Chinese Burn was—and probably still is—standard torture on school yards nation-wide: a two-handed grip is taken by the torturer on his victim's wrist and then he twists his hands in opposite directions, stretching and twisting the skin.

Mrs. Hunt was furious when we walked shamefacedly home with the girls. 'What about you boys?', she demanded continually. 'Where were you? Why did you let them?'

We pretended to read Roger's comics; there is a time for the truth and this was not it.

'Next time, you come here for me. I want to know. You boys come right here for me.'

Mrs. Hunt would sort them out. We read on; it was easier said than done, and Mrs. Hunt couldn't be with us *all* the time—we knew reprisals could be worse than ordinary battle. We males shifted anxiously while Mrs. Hunt made tea, little knowing what seed she had sown.

For there was yet another gang, older and more sophisticated than the rest: Ezzie Harold's gang, more secret, with no girls. Within a year—loyalties being what they are—I was to have disbanded my own and transferred to his, for Ezzie was a dashing figure, dazzling on the football field and handsome with it. Ezzie's gang was eventually metamorphosed into one of those secret societies so beloved in *The Wizard, Hotspur* or *Champion*—the Four Aces. Ezzie was of course the ace of football; Richard Evans the ace of cycling; Alan Lewis the ace of running, and I, shamefully, though it was never held against me, the ace of lessons, useful for writing out the rules. God knows what we used to do at our secret meetings on the Lugg Meadows. At this time, the Four Aces were a hand still to be played. But Ezzie's present gang was organized and efficient.

Roger, Michael, the two sisters and I spent a lot of time on Castle Green in Hereford, a wonderful place to play. Real cannon on Hogg's Mount overlook the large keep, and though it has no castle and a bowling green lies in the centre, the steep banks on three sides are good fun—the one grassed, to roll down; the other bare earth between trees, to slide down. This day we chased, rolled, slid and hid all over the Green until it was almost dusk; there was something nice and new about sliding, hiding, rolling and chasing in company with the girls which had no possible connection with the smut and songs I had picked up in the bars. We rushed to catch the ice-cream kiosk before the doors shut and set out, tired and happy, for home. We ambled giggling down the passage into Castle Street, made farting noises from a safe distance at the stuck-up boys of the Cathedral School (whom, all unknowing, I would be joining in under six months) and passed through the back gate of the Town Hall into St. Owen Street where, to our disbelieving horror, we ran slap into Ezzie and his gang looking for amusement.

We ran for it. *I* anyway ran for it, hearing cries and pounding feet dart away as I ran in the opposite direction to the general flight, crafty as ever. I must have run a frantic two hundred yards before it dawned on me that I had no pursuer, so I turned and carefully made my way back to where I could see the Town Hall safely from the deepening shadows.

There was no sign of Roger and Michael, but the poor girls had been taken. Handsome Ezzie and his henchmen were crowded tight round them and they seemed past resistance—and yet I was thrilled to see the hint of a defiant grin on Liz's lips as they were jostled by the leering gang (I had often wondered what a 'leer' was; as soon as I saw one I knew at once). A silence fell and a partial stillness; I guessed they were trying to decide what to do with their captives. Would it be the Chinese Burn?

Evidently not. From the shadows near the War Memorial I saw the group mill about indecisively; then there was movement and laughter and another brave grin from both girls who then looked away, dissociating themselves. There was more leering; one of the girls shrugged daringly, and then, appallingly, they were being urged back towards Castle Green. Poor hostages of fortune, they didn't resist. My heart was very heavy and I came from the shadows as soon as possible. The Chinese Burn in the secret darkness of Castle Green; it was a horrible prospect. I anxiously quartered the area for my fellow cowards but they were nowhere to be seen, and suddenly I had no part to play. Disconsolately I made for home; it was getting late.

But even as I walked I became aware of my responsibilities; they were my friends. The least I could do was to go home via Commercial Street and see if Roger had gained safety. I changed direction. But what would Mrs. Hunt say this time? We had fled the field once again; she would be making tea ready for Roger and Liz and God knows where they were.

'Next time you come here for me.' Chinese Burn up by the cannon; Liz and Janet with the leerers. I had a duty, not ignoble. Mrs. Hunt must at least be told her daughter, and possibly Roger too, would be late. Outside the door I hung about, hoping Roger and Michael would suddenly appear to share the task. Late shoppers pushed past; the toy shop closed, and then the butchers. I sighed and rang the bell.

Mrs. Hunt knew at once. Something terrible had happened. I could see it in her face; she had seen it in mine. 'What's wrong?'

I shrugged and looked at my feet.

'Come in.' She shut the door and pushed me into the living room. Suddenly she knelt on one knee at my side and looked with tragic eyes into mine. 'There's been an accident.'

She said it, not me, but I was having a new experience. Mrs. Hunt was as dramatic as I was, and neither of us knew it. I dropped my eyes slowly from the intense stare. I said, slowly, 'Outside the Town Hall.'

She straightened with a swift litheness; her mouth parted slightly. She whispered, 'Town Hall?'

I nodded.

Her voice stayed a whisper: 'Liz? Roger?'

'I said, 'Liz.'

She said, 'Roger?'

I shrugged. Then it began to go wrong. Mrs. Hunt grabbed a disastrously handy coat and made for the door; I was just getting round to the bit about Ezzie and the gang. I called out, 'Liz won't be home for tea.'

And she was out of the door at speed, with a sort of wailing sound deep in her throat. The door slammed shut. I sighed. Alone in the Hunts' house I was redundant again: the tide of drama, gathering, had swept over, leaving me high and dry. I sat down and leafed through Roger's comics. Slowly, misgivings about what had just happened began filtering through. I began to wonder what would eventually happen, then I got scared and left.

I never remember visiting Roger's house again. It was some time before I came to appreciate the enormity of what I'd done, or to realize that the devilish happenings on Hogg's Mount were both tamer and much more exciting than the Chinese Burn. It turned out that Roger and Michael had been very brave and at least kept their respective sisters under surveillance.

The girls came alone to the Commercial's back yard a few days later while I was banging a tennis ball back and forth between a bat and the shed door. I flicked them a look from the side of my eyes and concentrated on the ball until Liz reached up and caught it.

'Why did you tell our mam we'd been run over?' It was a question asked in pure interest: no annoyance.

I said, 'I didn't.'

'You did.' She bounced the ball to Janet.

'I was going to tell her about Ezzie's gang.'

They exchanged a look above the bouncing ball.

'But she went before I could.'

They bounced the ball between them. I had that old familiar feeling of redundancy and dropped the bat to sit on the swing.

I said, 'She just went out.'

It seemed to suffice. They bounced the ball against the shed for some time until inevitably it vanished through the open top of the door. I sighed and levered myself from the swing; I sought the ball among the pile of coal in the corner, and suddenly everything went dark. I looked round.

Janet and Liz were in the shed with me but the door was shut behind them, top and bottom. I saw them in the dark near the coal. What was going to happen? Not the Chinese Burn, oh please. I said nothing. Liz moved closer; it was very quiet.

'It wasn't my fault.'

Liz spoke absently: 'Ezzie says he'll get you.'

I said nothing and Janet moved up. It was frightening and exciting. Something was going to happen. Janet's voice was unusually loud. 'Ezzie knows—'

Liz quieted her quickly. Whatever was going to happen was strange and secret. I felt tingly.

'Ezzie knows some good jokes.'

Liz said, softly, 'You've got to say "in bed" after what I say.'

I went on silently tingling.

' "Our Father which art in Heaven—" '

' "In bed".'

' "Hallowed be thy name—" '

' "In bed".'

' "Thy Kingdom come—' "

' "In bed".'

' "Thy will be done—" '

' "In bed".'

Silence. Janet said, 'Don't you get it?'

I said nothing.

'Don't you get it? Thy will be done in bed.'

I didn't get it and the strange excitement began to loosen and dwindle; we *all* became redundant. Then Liz opened the door and they went home, leaving a blank disappointment. I knew I'd let them down.

Thy will be done in bed. . . .

I guessed it was a joke and I guessed what sort of a joke, but to be done in bed was a phrase outside my experience: the pub jokes were more explicit or at least more colourful. To do someone in bed was too tame for me; I only guessed vaguely what it meant. And I had no idea at all what it may have been leading up to.

I found the ball in the coal and took it outside to bang harder and harder against the shed wall, angry with myself.

Presumably Mrs. Hunt merely thought I was deranged and I'm grateful that she didn't come in person to vent her distress on me. It was the first time my yen for the dramatic had involved anybody else, but I went on thumping the ball against the angles of the shed, glad but disappointed I had escaped whatever may have been going to happen to me in the secret darkness of the shed. Liz and Janet never came round again; I assumed they'd joined Ezzie's gang. He obviously had something that I didn't. The ball flew from the bat handle through the open top of the shed door. I let it lie in the coal and went in for dinner.

♫ Musical Marie

The May Fair in Hereford and the main streets clogged with a riot of noise, smell, sound and light.

At one end: the station where a few desultory booths led soon to the sick, giddy Rotor (when eventually dared into riding, you seemed to lie flat on your back while the circle of gapers revolved faster and faster round the top of your head). Outside the Commercial the Big Wheel, and that hopeless, helpless slide of the stomach as your chair slipped over the top. More booths—penny-rolling, pin-balling, rifles, coconuts—and then the naughty treat of two garish strip shows, the Dirty Gerties and the Hairy Maries, illogically side by gloriously tatty side and even more illogically (or by wicked planning?) slap outside the staid, disapproving stones of the Baptist chapel. The Gerties and Maries where, so the masters of ceremonies promised, everything would come off at the last show but never did; where bored ladies of indeterminate age, running to fat, rolled vast breasts above our sweating faces and vaster hips a foot or so from our hot eyes—one G-string and two tinselled stars from total inglorious nudity, with Ravel's *Bolero* winding tinnily round the tent, where the M.C.s conjured or flame-swallowed to give time for our nervous expectations to rise ('Do it tickle?' one scrumpied wit called out as the M.C. ran a flaming torch up his side and beneath a hairless armpit).

Moving on to High Town, the tempo slackened—swings, a slow roundabout for the kids, until the thrill of the Ghost Train:

dark groping unlimited, and apparently unnoticed by the screaming girls who had enough to cope with anyway in the way of spiders, skeletons, vampire and the damp horrific dangling webs. Into packed Commercial Street—a chaos of booths leading to High Town, the centrepiece. The carousel pranced here; madder animals ran furiously round the undulating Noah's Ark twenty yards away; and between the two, the Caterpillar ran (or in some years the Whizzer—terrifying speed at the end of whirling struts). Dodgems were a highlight in High Town. Dolls were sold, hats, floss was spun, apples toffeed, all to the deafening mix of loud, distorted music and the snarl of half a dozen generators linked to machinery by a mass of black, snaking cables beneath your staggering feet.

After High Town, the action was quieter; a Housey-Housey stall when the word bingo was still unknown. The Haunted House—more groping if you wanted, and if you didn't, you could stand in the street and watch its window where sudden rushes of air blew skirts waist-high. You could see a mermaid one year; the Biggest Rat in the World and the Two-Headed Calf every year. And then you were round the corner and into the last street. The boxing booth, the Wall Of Death—stages for heroes. And finally, participation again—the Helter-Skelter and the giant full-stop of the Chairaplanes, swinging you out high, fast and wide above the whirlpool of lights until they merged into one orange-white spectrum.

And that was the May Fair: I can have named less than half of it. Three-quarters of a glorious mile, emptying your pocket and not infrequently your stomach, into which you plunged at one end of the town, to emerge gasping, gaping, thrilled and outraged at the sheer difference of it all. Three days of grimy wonder and cheap illusion which began with the quiet creeping invasion of the lorries after midnight on the first Monday in May, and ended at eleven on Thursday (for me at least) outside the Baptist chapel, in the desperate hope that one random Hairy Marie at least might just keep, this year, last year's promise and shake herself free of stars and string, revealing at last whatever all was.

Our headmaster posted each year an invariable notice on the board at the beginning of the wonderful week:

It is possible to spend a very great deal of money at the Fair and have very little to show for it.

Well, that's all *he* knew; we recognized the thin Puritan whine even then.

Sid and I were seventeen and superior with it; intellectuals. He was the cynic, I the optimist. May Fair was of course beneath us both but we went nevertheless. We might take a ride or two—something to scoff at—before trading insults with a Fat Lady or Tattooed Man. We might enjoy a little mocking. It was all very civilized. If our minor public school was giving us little else, it was jacking us up a notch or two to where we could peer down, gently smiling, and scatter pretentious ironies on the less fortunate crowd. We knew who Eliot and Dylan Thomas were and both the Lawrences—so there. In brief, Sid and I were insufferable, and somewhere between the Haunted House and Giant Rat we became aware of Marilyn and her friend.

Marilyn was the sex-symbol of our Sixth Form. Certain favoured few of the boarders had Been Out with Marilyn and walked around for the next day or so with a highly enigmatic smile on sealed lips; one had been seen, grimly red-faced, hanging about Boots's counter waiting for the male assistant to be free. In those pre-permissive days, such a mild erotic breeze was all our fantasies needed to explode into flame. Cool, slim Marilyn with her gently carnal smile—a sixteen-year-old Bacall to us hopeful, hopeless Bogarts—was driving us crazy. (Within the year I would have twice Been Out with Marilyn. But no enigmatic smile for me. Each time I walked her home she made the final dash along her wooded drive to the front door with such skill that I wondered she never took up Olympic sprinting.)

Anne, her friend, lacked Marilyn's looks or style, but the Sixth Form was uneasy about her; her reputation grew amongst us as some sort of primal devouring force, an earth mother demanding sacrifice—she was a large girl.

So when Sid and I—somewhere along Broad Street—
realized we were being followed by Marilyn and her friend, we
affected disinterest and a little annoyance but were, in fact,
terrified. Marilyn's perfection and Anne's reputation were too
wild to be governed by our inexperienced grasping. The issues
were too complicated: what if our ironies fell flat? What if we
should fail? And which of us would have to have Marilyn's
friend?

The pursuit became increasingly embarrassing. Obvious
flight was out of the question. We ignored the presences always
at our backs, giggles and all, but the presences remained. We
went in to trade a few half-hearted ironies with the Fat Lady
but our barbs were blunt against her massive folds of flesh, and
when we moved back into the crowds the Furies were waiting.
The pursuit lurched into ignominy. Paper balls stuffed with
sawdust were bounced on elastic strings against our solidly
turned backs and if the symbolism escaped me then, I wince at it
now. Into the Nelson we went for a beer, out into Broad Street
we came again and there they were. Our bluff was being called
and we were running out of evasions—God knew what we
would have to suffer when the story leapt from the Girls' High
School to ours.

Desperate situations dictate desperate remedies. We were
aware that some entertainment was running at the Kemble
Theatre, just behind the Rat and Two-Headed Sheep. Exactly
who Musical Marie was, or what marathon she was attempting
we did not know, but in the familiar auditorium lay darkness,
salvation, not to mention four widely-spaced exits. Sid and I
paid our shillings and walked in. The theatre was disastrously
well lit, and on the stage a plump motherly lady in a long gown
was playing a piano. At her side sat a man of middle age in a
dinner jacket, chatting. Her playing was nothing special; it
was the sort you might once have heard in a pub on a Saturday
night, the sort my mother managed so spectacularly well; I was
quite used to it. Someone approached the stage and talked a
while with the lady and gentleman. Sid and I found two seats
in the sparse audience. As Marilyn and her friend came giggling

c

into the Kemble, the man in the dinner jacket moved to a microphone stand and talked to us.

Musical Marie was attempting, right here in the Kemble Theatre, Hereford, to break the world record for non-stop piano playing. She had begun the previous evening, Monday, and would, if successful, conclude the venture at 11 p.m. on Saturday night. He smiled, moved back from the mike and quietly sat again at Marie's side; she threw a quick smile round us all. We were transfixed. God almighty! This woman had been playing that piano for almost 24 hours and had four solid days ahead of her.

These were the days before the *Guinness Book of Records*. We had never come into living contact with anything quite so surrealist. We gaped at the stage, oblivious of the repeated giggles from two rows behind and the occasional sharp tap of sawdust balls on the backs of our heads. These grew more infrequent, and when we looked around, remembering the reason for our presence in the Kemble, Marilyn and her friend had gone. Musical Marie broke into the zither tune from *The Third Man*. Sid and I settled back in our seats. Marie smiled.

Cruel daylight and the rain that May Fair always brought with it put the prince back inside the toad. Unused, unloved, unopened, May Fair was a sly dirty monster flopped dead in our streets. When we skirted the carcass at the end of morning school, clutches of children wandered, desolate at the Fair's apparent death, poking at the remains. But Sid and I were full of purpose. No slick epigrams about the dead fair this morning. Shillings paid, we were setting in the Kemble almost before the school bell had stopped ringing.

Inside, there had been a change. Marie sat at the piano, playing much as she had been 16 hours before, but the dramatic mood had given way to a more relaxed one. For a start, there were barely a dozen of us in the auditorium and the working lights were on, emphasizing the rows of emptiness. Typically for us shy Border people, none dared sit nearer the stage than the back half-dozen rows, but two or three strangers—probably part of Marie's entourage—leant over the orchestra pit, chatting. On stage, Marie had changed into a less formal dress (how?) and the manager's dinner jacket had given way to shirt sleeves and slacks. He held his place at Marie's side, smiling, chatting. At one particular moment, one of the group must have mentioned us, for suddenly all turned to survey us in silence; then the manager must have joked, for they all laughed, but not cruelly, before turning back into their tight, privileged group, though Marie's eyes stayed on us, smiling gently. Then she struck a bum chord and before I had time to mention it to Sid, she had used it to slide expertly into another number. Well, after 40 hours or so, she was entitled to a bum chord now and then. She shook a rueful head down at her fingers and I thrilled to her professionalism.

But then came an unexpected turn-off. The manager came to his microphone. He told us again that Marie was attempting the world record right here in Hereford. He welcomed us, hoped we would feel free to request numbers, hoped we would feel free to come forward and meet Marie personally, hoped we would come again. So far so good; Sid and I held a quick whispered debate whether we should meet Marie, as invited, as the lunch hour was wearing on. But then the matter was decided for us.

'Ladies and gentlemen—Marie, like all of us, is only human and when you've got to go, you've got to go!'

He smiled widely and the small group of strangers up front moved from the auditorium by a door which we knew would lead them on stage. What was he talking about?

'Ladies and gentlemen—the screens will now be placed round Marie for a minute or two. She will of course continue to play.'

The faithful few came on stage with hospital screens which were carefully placed around the piano.

Sid said, 'Christ!'

'Ladies and gentlemen—we shall now be closing the front curtains until Marie's toilet is performed. If any lady would care to come on stage she will see for herself this is no subterfuge.'

He smiled enquiringly out to the back of the theatre where

the twelve of us stared rigidly to the front in the primeval fear
of twitching unconsciously at the auction and finding ourselves
the mortified possessors of something unlooked for, monstrous.
The curtains closed.

Sid and I said together, 'Christ!' Our surrealism strictly
excluded defecation, and anyway, as we agreed hastily, the
lunch hour must be almost over; neither of us had eaten.

Outside, the Fat Lady, fully clothed, was taking the wraps
from the Giant Rat stall. She stared at us incuriously and lit a
cigarette.

That afternoon, while I was supposed to be writing an essay
on Balzac, alone in the common room, my thoughts kept circling
round Marie, sore-fingered surely by now, not two hundred
yards away in the Kemble. Who was Musical Marie? What did
she do in real life? Who was the manager? The group at the
edge of the stage, who were they?

I had one marked down as Marie's doctor, as surely she would
need one. He was about sixty, moustached, in a blue suit; he
had an air of cynical world-weariness which put Sid's attempts
well in the shade. I could imagine the steel eyes focusing
sharply in amusement at the weird by-lane up which his
Hippocratic oath had led them.

The manager was not her husband. My first neat thoughts
had been unravelled the instant he had thrown out his monstrous
invitation to any lady in the audience. It was tinged with the
commercial, the sensational. What husband would put his wife
to the degradation of a public shit, for God's sake? I could
almost hear the discussion at the planning stage: he adamantly
in favour, on the grounds of good business, she quietly protesting, lifting gentle eyes to the Doc for support but finding only
cynical amusement and a brief shrug.

But Marie herself? And the two younger men? Before I could
get to work on them, Sid came in, his essay finished, to ask about
the evening. I was evasive, didn't know if I'd be going out or
not; maybe see him round the streets. Sid and I were good
friends; he probably thought I couldn't face another possible
confrontation with Marilyn and her friend (who, incidentally,

had been putting the dirt round the Girls' High School with
zest). He was right, of course; he'd feel the same. In any case,
he didn't press the point. In truth, Marilyn and her friend were
already out of my mind and into the cruellest, crudest pub
jokes I knew—and I knew some beauties—that would teach
them. I had more intense obsessions now: I wanted Marie to
myself, and the intervening hour would be full of sore-fingered
fatigue, embarrassment above a vista of ivory and strangers'
faces.

I suppose it must have been the first time I had walked
virtually the length of May Fair with no interest in it. Wednesday
night was the second of its three, and market day too, when the
fair was always packed. I watched the couples on the Big Wheel
as I changed from school uniform in my bedroom, but they
seemed hysterical and boring. Past the Baptist chapel I strolled
with never a glance at the Maries and Gerties warming up the
crowds before their performances. I skirted the mobs in Commercial Street and High Town, moving through quieter rain-
soaked ways to come to the Cathedral close. I passed the jostle,
smells and screams between the Haunted House and the Giant
Rat, paid my shilling at the Kemble box-office and took a seat
half-way back. I knew I should never approach nearer.

Marie was in another dress, very formal, and amazingly her
playing seemed not to have deteriorated. Certainly she was the
same: the smiles, the gentle nodding into the half-darkened
auditorium. Stage lighting and an audience had sharpened the
sense of theatre again. A new touch too at the side of the stage:
a board with the hours she had been playing chalked up—48
now, leaving 75 to go. It was a shock to realize she was not even
half-way. Another new touch at the piano's legs: a basket of
flowers, from a well-wisher, I guessed—neither the manager or
doctor would send flowers to her.

Marie was alone on the stage and I looked round for the
Manager, annoyed that he should leave his place at her side, and
found him sitting in the audience, laughing with two women
and a man; no sign of any other members of the group. I had
a sudden disloyal vision of the doctor, plastered in the City Arms

or the Dragon. Where were the others? What if she fainted, got cramp, needed the vile screens? I needn't have worried. The manager gave a swift glance at the stage, scribbled on an envelope, smiled at his companions in the stalls and threaded his way through empty seats to the door on the stage where he appeared a few seconds later, to place the note on the envelope before Marie.

He moved to the mike, and announced that Musical Marie was attempting to break the world record right here in Hereford, that we were welcome now and would be even more welcome next time, that requests for Marie were gladly received and that indeed she was about to play a medley for Mr. and Mrs. Some-one-or-other of Tupsley, Hereford. Marie smiled, nodded and played about four numbers well, with those scales, arpeggios, chords between the tunes which change the key and used to be so popular. At the end, clapping broke out, feebly at first, but then warm and loud. Marie's face lit up and while the left hand doodled up and down the lower register, the right hand waved and blew us a kiss.

It was a charming moment which lit our faces too. A sudden warmth came over us and for the first time, a party atmosphere blossomed, very different from our earlier voyeuristic curiosity. The manager thanked us for the applause and told us how much Marie liked Hereford, and us, her audiences (she nodded). He told us how much she was looking forward to shopping in Hereford's fine shops, looking round the fine Cathedral and to meeting some of us over a drink when it was all over and several good gins wouldn't either do something funny to the music or make her want to spend a penny. Thank you.

There was some dutiful giggling and more clapping. Marie stared at her fingers—and suddenly she swept us up in a net of chords and we were into a sing-song: 'Lily of Laguna'; 'If You Were the Only Girl in the World'; 'Keep Right on to the End of the Road'; 'You Are My Sunshine'. Sid came in and found me and we sang our hearts out. The theatre filled maybe a quarter of its seats. When we left, I knew she would see the evening through, she'd be okay until I could get to her next lunch hour; she would be almost half-way through the ordeal then. Several of the audience had come forward and were clustered at the edge of the stage, talking up to Marie, who smiled, nodded, laughed. In the foyer we met the two men and the doctor coming in and I turned a very sour look full on them—back to your posts, Marie needs you.

'That's her doctor,' I shouted to Sid as we came into the Fair.

'How d'you know?'

'I heard him say,' I lied, wondering why I needed to lie.

But the monster had come alive again, and we had to fight all the way down to the chapel to be in time for the last show. The M.C. promised everything was going to come off tomorrow night.

Thursday—and the last of May Fair for another year. Traditionally it was the busiest of the days but I found it frenzied and remote; for a start, Hereford folk could easily have too much of a good thing and by Thursday night our senses were battered, our pockets emptied. The Fair people too were different—in need of rest and faced with the exhausting prospect of having to pack and be away from the streets by next morning in time for the Council workers to clean up the sordid detritus. The only genuine mourners for the Fair's annual decease were the younger kids, and they went mad, sensing the passing of magic from their desperate grasp, crazy for the last drop of dragon's blood before the beast faded at midnight.

At lunchtime it lay silent and washed out, conserving its resources for the final frantic writhe. The horror was that tiredness was also creeping on stage at the Kemble. I asked the girl at the cash desk how Marie was and she simply shook her head. Jesus—I was in the auditorium before my shilling hit the till. Had the word got round? There must have been fifty of us sitting in silent misery.

'She'll get her second breath,' I heard a neighbour whisper to her husband.

'She needs it,' I heard him reply.

64 hours gone; 59 hours to go. A grey tide of exhaustion had

quietly crept across the stage overnight. Marie's actual appearance was only marginally the worse: her shoulders were more slumped and her head further down, but her daytime dress was bright and from time to time the smile still wandered across the pit to us; it was her playing that had suffered. Gone the sparkling runs from bass to treble; gone the grasshopper ragtime beat; gone the vigour and the party mood. Slow, sombre chords hung like shrouds round a barely discernible melody, and 59 hours to go. More changes: more flowers on stage and on the piano, two jugs—one of water and one of orange squash. I realized I had never seen her eat. Downstage stood a settee covered in bright floral material and on it, slumped, the biggest shock of all: the grey-faced manager, leaden with fatigue.

Marie's fingers slipped badly, ruining the tune, and she stared down at them, puzzled. Her head shook imperceptibly, much as the cash-desk girl's had done. No attempt this time to modulate into another number. She jangled on, compounding the error until none of us could recognize what she was playing. And still the manager stared glassily down into the pit, drained of energy. Just when Marie needed a lift, a reassuring glance, a light chuckle and easy word or two, he was letting her down. Marie arrived at the end of the grotesque tune and chorded non sequiturs in the bass while she poured the orange drink into a glass. Where was the manager? His job this, surely? Where was the doctor?

Then suddenly somebody applauded. At first it was despicable, even mocking, and I swung a sour look towards the sound. But the woman banging inappropriate hands was obviously sincere. The two sounds hung in the air: slow chords, bad chords, any chords and the loud brash clapping. I saw then it was not a response to Marie's fingers but to her spirit and my heart jumped, filled. I clapped madly. The man and woman at my side joined us. Then three girls in front. Ten seconds more and the Kemble rang to applause that had more of hysteria than appreciation.

Marie put down the glass and peered out at us, bewildered. More important, the manager snapped out of his reverie. Marie

smiled. We beat our hands desperately. The manager reached
for his coat and stood.

Then magically, emotionally, Marie's left hand began the
familiar bounce and the treble notes rippled. She was into 'You
Are My Sunshine' again and if it lacked the zip of last night,
no matter. She belted it. Her foot pumped pedals and her
shoulders went back as her head rose triumphantly.

> *'You make me happy when skies are grey'*

Her lips were moving. She was singing. Dear God, Marie was
singing!

> *'You'll never know, dear, how much I love you'*

The manager was singing!

> *'Please don't take my sunshine away.'*

And one more time, all together now, bigger, better:

> *'The other night, dear, as I lay dreaming,*
> *I dreamt that you were by my side . . .'*

And now we were all singing, clapping in rhythm:

> *'Then I awoke, dear, and you had left me.*
> *So I hung my head and cried.'*

Then arpeggios, inexact but unmistakable, a key change to a
right-hand ripple and—unbelievably—the rollicking 'Knees
Up, Mother Brown'. We clapped excitedly to her beat. 'I told
you!' my neighbour cried.

> *'Under the table you must go . . .'*

And now the manager at his mike: 'Ladies and gentlemen—'
I prayed he wouldn't ruin the moment and he didn't. Marie was
attempting the non-stop piano-playing record right here this
week in Hereford. We were welcome; he hoped we'd come again.

Oh God, I couldn't stand much more of this. I was used to
the familiar turbulence of pub life, but Marie and her record
were killing me. As I staggered into the aisle, I saw the doctor

and one of the men bearing a tray of food towards the stage door. Thank God, thank God, thank God, and then I was out into the street, gulping damp air and late for afternoon school.

Who then was Musical Marie? I could not pin her down. She obstinately remained a blank space at the centre of this drama revolving round her, a gently smiling enigma as the lesser mortals involved fell one by one into place as the week wore on. I had sussed out the older of the two attendants: he was a menial, merely—a fetcher and carrier in his thirties, good-looking in a bland, easy-going way, I knew brain when I saw it and, by God, I didn't see it there. The younger hadn't revealed himself to me yet but there was time. In any case, he didn't matter. It was Marie who was troubling me.

She was complaisant; she was warm; she had courage. She was concerned with her appearance but shat in semi-public. She could play. But what did it all add up to? I spent another afternoon idly kicking Blazac around while my concentration, such as it was, stayed with Marie. Sid came in from watching athletics at about zero minus $54\frac{1}{2}$ with the news that Raymond was taking Marilyn out tonight, that we'd not done well in the athletics and that the master in charge had asked him did I never, ever turn up to encourage my House (the answer was not if I could help it). Oh well, small beer, all of it, compared with those deathly chords and the jump as my heart turned over with Marie's applause. I told Sid some of the lunchtime drama and we agreed to meet for a quick look at the Fair that night but to spend most of the evening in the Kemble. I was going to call in to see Marie on the way home but I didn't tell him. I was getting possessive about my heroine.

The atmosphere in the Kemble, that night, was grim. I'd guess that the marked effect of the overnight tiredness must have alarmed the whole crew. No flowers tonight but more drinks on the piano. Marie was formally dressed again, the manager was in his dinner jacket and the doctor, the menial and the other man were all on stage. The theatre itself was about one-third full. Determination was the watchword and we looked on, guiltily fixed between the fear and the hope of disaster. 73 hours had gone and 50 were to go. The visit was a non-event and Sid must have wondered it I'd invented my lunchtime account of the record attempt in its death-throes. Marie's spirit and professionalism were entirely dominant; she was pacing herself with music that demanded little. Incredibly we heard 'Happy Birthday to You' and looked idly round for the recipient but there was none.

In fact there was no involvement with the audience at all. Marie kept her head down—not in the slump of defeat but in watchful concentration, daring her hands to make a mess of it. No smiles came out to us, no waves, no kisses. Marie was doing a job. I admired, but felt let down; we might just as well not have been there. The manager asked for no requests and made no announcements. The party was over; we were being excluded. The mystery man sat at Marie's side; occasionally his mouth moved but drew no response from her. He looked suddenly at his watch, rose, and the doctor took his place. The piano, intimidated by Marie's brooding attention, seemed quieter and played a cut-down version of 'In a Monastery Garden'—I thought we had heard it before as we took our seats. The menial checked times with the manager and took a cloth to the board: 74 gone, 49 to go. The doctor poured something green (lime juice?) into a glass which Marie drank as the left hand pushed down sensible chords and the audience shifted uneasily. Something had gone and we were feeling its loss.

A couple of drunks shouted from the foyer and the auditorium doors suddenly swung them in, grinning and noisy. We craned round—and then back, eager for drama, to see what the unexpected intrusion would provoke on stage. The manager, menial and mystery man stared briefly out: we could see the manager considering if the drunks would be any threat to Marie, but she seemed not to have noticed, and the heads moved away uninterested—the drunks were irrelevant. They must have felt so too, for the doors banged once more and they were gone.

Others were going too. Sid and I looked at each other, nodded and moved quietly towards the exit. Where had all the drama gone? As the doors closed quietly behind us, we heard

'Happy Birthday to You' creep quietly down the theatre. Like the drunks, I felt irrelevant and let down. I wouldn't bother tomorrow lunchtime.

In the streets the Fair was careering through its last few hours. We stood on the Kemble steps, looking despondently on the wild scene. Others of Marie's recent audience passed us. 'Nothing much,' one said. And that was right. Bloody Marie, bloody manager, bloody doctor, menial and mystery man. One human spirit was doing public battle with a three-days-fatigued brain, a 74-hours-weakened body with all the attendant obstacles, and the sum total of all this brave endeavour? 'Happy Birthday to You'.

Sid and I rushed into the fray. Chairaplanes we rode, Noah's Ark, Dodgems and Big Wheel. We deflated the Fat Lady with one combined sour look. We saw Sheep, boxing, Rotor and Rat. Up and down the Fair we toiled with occasional brief pauses in favourite pubs. We rode the Dodgems again and saw the very last performance of the Hairy Maries—and this year, as last year, as every year, nothing untoward came off; it was stars and stripes for ever. I staggered into the Commercial at half-past midnight, broke, boozed and battered. There were a few last crates of empties to be taken down to the cellar. Caleb, our barman, enjoying a last quiet drink, asked if I'd had a good time and I expended what was left of my sour look on him as I lurched by and heard his quiet laughter as I humped the crates down.

And ridiculously, when I got up the next morning, May Fair had gone and the streets were clean. Hereford, as though ashamed of its untypical May madness, had somehow managed to pretend it had all never happened. I cycled through streets which only hours before had barely contained the thousands of citizens hell-bent on fun and saw only other schoolboys and the occasional car. It seemed very quiet. We had the bleak, dazed looks of survivors as we wound our way through the blank city.

School, too, was bleak. Was it the Fair or was it us? Most of us had seen the Fair out, and we had a tired unwashedness about us. I was not the only one to fail to hand in the Balzac essay and to ensure the gibes of Jo, our French master. A lazy voice from the back advised '*Cherchez la femme*' as I stumbled through my apologies. Bloody Marilyn ... or did he mean Marie? Bloody Marie, anyway. But I couldn't help wondering how those fingers were making out with 38 hours to go. 38 hours: the time was appreciable now; just over a day and a half: tomorrow was the end—if she got there. When Jo asked me to carry on the translation I'd even forgotten what we were translating and had to undergo the whole gibe and *Cherchez la femme* bit all over again. 'Sorry, sir?'

Sid sniggered at my side.

Of course, I did go to the Kemble at lunchtime but nothing had changed except the dress and the dinner jacket. The same grim concentration crowded out the dozen or so of us there to watch. I didn't stay— anyway I had an essay to finish. 34 hours to go; she would make it. Another man had joined the entourage but I couldn't have cared less. Would I come tonight? Possibly. Sid was playing football; I had work to do—three nights' work. The bloody Fair. Could our headmaster be right? No: it had been worth it. 'So Tired'—Marie was playing it. Surely we'd have a smile for something so appropriate? No. I went to lunch.

So much for complacency. The Kemble on Friday evening was a bad dream. Musical Marie had given up being musical. There was barely a tune left seeping down from tired brain to numbed fingers. Muted chords fumbled round melodies heard only in her dimming mind, quite inaudible to us. Ghostly snatches of treble notes wandered inappropriately into her reverie and a crazy off beat bass occasionally broke through at the wrong times. The music of hell. A mist of fatigue had settled over Musical Marie. What we were hearing was the genuine disintegration of a personality in eight octaves.

The sight was as desperate as the sound. Marie seemed to have collapsed inwardly: her face, head, shoulders were poured low over the keys. The sagging face was maybe the hardest to bear—when she struggled to turn a travesty of a smile on us, the silence in the auditorium was total, horrified. Her entourage were bunched close round her, silent also, giving what support they could simply by being there. But she seemed unaware of them—unaware almost of everything but the necessity to keep sounds struck from the piano.

I watched hopelessly: to fail NOW . . . For Musical Marie to hit non-stop notes for 97 hours and fail on virtually the last day . . . The enormity of *all* record-breaking flooded in on me: the loneliness of the long-distance runner; the grotesque flapping form of Jim Peters in the Olympic marathon; Lindbergh over the Atlantic. To me such feats had always been remote, tidied up in newspaper and radio reports. Now I was seeing the reality: the true sequence of events as one by one the skills dried up under the enormous pressure. And the sheer loneliness . . . Musical Marie had nothing much left now but the knowledge that blistered fingertips must continue to drop on hard piano keys. We were hearing her exhausted spirits drawing on the little that was left of her strength. To fail NOW . . .

No sudden appreciative burst of applause would save her now; no requests from Tupsley. We were out of it. I realized that what I'd been seeing over the last 24 hours was a complete progression. At the start, we in the auditorium had a part to play: we encouraged, challenged, fed her. Inexorably the focus had moved to the stage where her group had taken over the task of reinforcing her will. Even that focus had shifted. The whole ridiculous, wonderful venture was dependent upon what resources Marie herself could now call on. Those resources too were narrowing. What, in the end, would be left? Where would the final fire burn? In the fingers? The brain? The heart?

And suddenly I wanted her to give it up; give it all up. It was not worth it. I wanted the curtains to close on her. I wanted Marie to be taken from the piano to the settee. I wanted her clean and refreshed so that I might see her, after long deep rest, shopping in Greenlands, looking at the Cathedral, where I might approach her and say, 'Well done, you nearly made it, it was a good attempt—congratulations.' And if I who was not suffering in public on the Kemble stage could feel that, what temptations must Marie have felt? She was out on her backside with $25\frac{1}{2}$ hours to go. Give up, give up, give up. The more that cruel courage drove her on, the more poignant must be the loss when strength eventually deserted her. What if she should collapse in 24 hours' time, 90 minutes short? How could she bear it? How could any of us bear it?

Someone approached the stage who looked local and the manager came slowly to talk with him. A short conversation and each returned to his post. The manager leant over Marie and spoke. The slumped head nodded briefly. She had been given a request. God almighty, how could anyone do that to her? And yet . . . The hope flickered that the magic might work again. For what seemed a long time there was no appreciable change in the random complexities of sound, and then, slowly, slowly, the rhythms settled and harmonies moved into a barely recognizable pattern. Marie was obviously thinking she was playing *something*, but what? The tempo remained sombre, deathly, but somewhere a tune was being carved out. . . . 'And sunshine we'd have every day'. 'We would live all alone . . .' And then it had gone again. But we knew the tune now and her struggles seemed to approximate to the melody in our heads. '. . . Queen on a throne. If I had my way . . .' Then a parody of modulations into another key. Christ, it was grotesque. And then the unmistakable sly zither from *The Third Man*, but no zip, no Viennese confidence. The notes jingled and jangled in slow, haphazard sequence and, half-way through, Marie lost interest. The tune faltered, changed shape and the accompaniment dithered. In a second she was back with the dead soul music and there were no more requests.

One emotional moment remains in my mind of that terrible evening. I had gone to the theatre at nine, intending to stay until eleven when the significant 24 hours would be chalked on the board. At a particularly bad time, about 10.30, when it seemed likely that any final drop of strength would dry up, the mystery man put an arm round Marie and hugged her gently. She looked up to him but her face was turned away and we could not see her response; only she laid her head on his arm for a while and it came to me that he was her son.

I saw the final day marked up and left quietly. I didn't know if I expected to find her playing, the next day, and, to be frank, I didn't care. I'd seen a human being slowly running down and I'd heard sounds that had chilled. The week had focused itself entirely inside Marie and released me from involvement, but it was a hollow gain and I felt so tired that I walked the bike home. I had worried that I wouldn't be able to see Marie on Saturday until the evening (morning school and then a late rugby match in Worcester), but now . . . I didn't know. The journey to Commercial Road seemed to take a long time.

Saturday came bright and sharp. I felt good. At school I finished the Balzac essay and spent a further free period after break chatting in one of the boarding-house studies: my Marilyn jokes went down well. At midday, I and the others who were to play at Worcester caught the coach and eventually had a good game which ended in a draw. After tea we wandered round Worcester before leaving for Hereford about six o'clock and it was nearly eight when we drew up at the school. I was tired and bruised; in Deanery House I begged a long soak in a bath and relaxed. The study fags came down from the film in big school to make us coffee. A master looked in for a chat. I wandered over to the common room about half-past nine to meet Sid and find out if Marie were still playing. If not, we'd go with others down to the Nelson or the Bridge and spend the rest of the evening there.

Sid was anxious to leave for the Kemble at once. The crowds were gathering into a queue. I was amazed. Yes, Marie was still playing: he'd looked in about four. Yes, she was fine, and yes, of course you could tell what she was playing. Come on—the place would be packed—and what did I mean about not being able to tell what she was playing?

We paid two shillings each for entrance but I would have paid anything. The atmosphere was enthusiastic and we were happy to queue. The stalls where we had sat during the week were already full and we were lucky to get seats high in the balcony, for at least half the queue behind us was going to have to stand or suffer disappointment. We thumped down the tipped seats and took in the scene.

Back to pure theatre again. Marie in black, with stones sparkling the length of the long gown. The manager, smiling in dinner jacket, and the doctor, menial and son in dinner jackets too. An addition on the stage: a young woman, very attractive, beaming at Marie's side, the son's arm round her. His wife? Marie's daughter, and the son a son-in-law after all? Never mind. Flowers everywhere. A packed audience, noisy, expectant, good-humoured. The menial chalked up 122 gone, 1 hour to go. A cheer from us: I'd never seen the Kemble so full. Doors closed at the back of the balcony; standing downstairs only. Brilliant! And brilliant in a close overhead spotlight, most brilliant of all in sparkling black—Musical Marie, smiling.

It was not the smile of the early week and her make-up was heavy to obliterate the ravages of five days. Her eyes were puffed up—there was no hiding that—but she was still there. God almighty, still there and still playing. Had the daughter's arrival made all the difference? Who would have sent for her? I saw it all. The urgent telegram sent from the Post Office opposite the theatre; the knock of the telegram boy in some far-off town; the hasty packing of an overnight case and the lip-biting journey to sleeping Hereford; the rousting out of an all-night taxi and the rushing to the theatre. I saw the arrival in the bleak early hours and the tearful reunion, the two alone together, the child strengthening the parent and the slow confidence beginning to return as new resources were tapped and fresh strength flowed into numb body and mind. God, this was the real thing. I realized suddenly that I had no idea how any of this had affected the playing, so I shut down my spinning emotions and listened. Sid leant over to say something and I shut him up.

It wasn't marvellous but it was there. Quietly beneath the hubbub of Herefordians, tired tunes were obstinately beating out into the final fifty minutes. My heart heaved and I hoped I wouldn't cry—one of the most emotional hours of my life was under way.

A smiling menial rubbed the board clear and wrote in a firm hand 45 minutes. Another cheer; applause. A weary, warm smile from Marie and a hug from the daughter. I was sure now that Marie was doing it all for her and the son-in-law. A new house? Maybe a baby on the way—no sign of that, but it must be something of the sort.

Marie was into a settled pattern of playing now: a quiet, easy tune—'Tea for Two' maybe—and then a few minutes of chords. I sensed the growing triumph. Excitement was infectious; smiles were everywhere. An usherette bore flowers onto the stage which the daughter darted down to collect while we cheered and applauded anew. She held them up to us and carried them to the piano. Wonderful Marie smiled and blew us a kiss. I clapped like a maniac, surprising even Sid, and then there were 30 minutes to go and we all set each other off again, frenzied, hysterical.

The manager moved to the microphone and we fell silent. Musical Marie, he said, was now in her final thirty minutes. He thanked us for our support, our flowers, our warmth. He particularly thanked those who had come to the theatre in the small hours to help Marie through the difficult times.

Suddenly yet another image of Marie had stepped up for appraisal. Marie the uniter. I realized that others had been as involved as I—more involved: involved enough to want to call in, probably tired themselves, after long night shifts, or on the way to hard, early work. And in Hereford of all places. Marie had sparked feelings in us that a week before would have seemed impossible. It was only right that the whole of Hereford appeared to be gathered to share her triumph. But why Hereford? A sudden thought—she didn't come from Hereford. Was it for the May Fair crowds, now so amazingly metamorphosed into this warm-hearted, well-dressed audience? Maybe the Kemble had been the only medium-sized theatre available for the one week. Why Hereford? Never mind. To Hereford she had come and we were ecstatic for her. Another thought, crueller. What of the current record-holder whose similar torment even now counted as nothing? Who and where was he (or she)? I saw him pacing his rooms in Novgorod or wherever, desperate for the cable rushed in by his manager: HEREFORD MAY 8, MUSICAL MARIE ONE TWO THREE HOURS NONSTOP STOP. I saw his despair, saw him sink into his chair, saw his manager rush to the vodka bottle.

Meanwhile the menial was on the move. 15 minutes and another storm of cheering; another wave and smile across the darkness. And then a strange mood: silence. A smiling silence carried Marie to her triumph, savouring success with her, feeling it for her, recognizing we would not see its like again. I recalled the week: the joys and disappointments, the despairs and the hopefulness, the anxieties. I had experienced something I knew would be unique. We listened sadly to the final few minutes of the jangled chords and rhythms—not music now of a dead soul but the quiet conclusions to an impossible venture confidently concluded. Marie was sailing into port.

The son-in-law and daughter moved to flank their magnificent mother. The menial took his duster to the board. The manager walked to the microphone and took out a pocket watch. The doctor came on stage with a bottle of champagne and six glasses on a tray. The silence was beginning to break; rushes of sound swept back and forth, growing, growing. The menial raised his duster; the manager raised his hand.

'Ladies and gentlemen—in a few seconds Musical Marie will have broken the world record of one hundred and twenty-two hours non-stop piano playing. I ask you all to stand.'

We stood. In complete silence. And suddenly, brilliantly, wonderful magnificent Marie struck a tremolo bass chord— heavy, low, triumphant. 'God Save Our Gracious Queen'.

Oh Christ, Oh Christ, I wept and sang. All round us the crowds lifted hearts and sang the national anthem. I've been to Cardiff Arms Park, heard Wembley, but never anything like this. We wished long life to the Queen but the queen was Marie.

> *'Send her victorious,*
> *Happy and glorious . . .'*

Sid and I sang as we'd never sung before and by the time the last line was half sung, the cheering, the clapping and shouting had taken over. Down came the manager's arm. Off came the final chalk mark; out came the champagne cork and round Marie went her daughter's arms. The Kemble was large: 1500 of us screamed and shouted Marie's triumph. It went on and on.

Bless her, she could not stand but our love would have lifted her anyway. The group carried her gently to the settee. She sat, eyes closed, unmoving as the triumph drove on; we must have cheered for fully five minutes. The glasses on stage were lifted and drained but Marie never moved. The tumult weakened in sudden apprehension but then the eyes opened and smiled, the warm mouth curved to us and we screamed love back at her. Oh God, she could not hold the glass. The manager held it to her lips and she drank slowly, gratefully, devotionally, a communicant. The menial brought her the microphone. A torrent of sssshhhing and Marie spoke. Her voice was low, empty, curiously refined, dwindling occasionally to a whisper.

'Ladies and gentlemen, thank you and bless you all. We shall always remember Hereford and the wonderful support you have given us in my successful attempt to break my own world record. Thank you, and bless you once again.'

Her *own* world record? Just a moment . . . But then she stood and moved heavily forward and we were all clapping and shouting again. The curtains closed behind her and she blew kisses, waved and smiled. She took small, unsteady steps and walked behind the curtain, gone from us for ever.

The theatre took time to empty but nobody minded. A perfect, long drama had been shaped and played out right here in Hereford, and real-life at that. We waited, glowing, for our turn to move through the doors and on to the stairs.

'What was that about it being her own record?' I asked Sid.

Sid shrugged and we pressed down into the crowded foyer. We felt exhausted, drained of all emotion, and it seemed a general reaction—everybody was dazed with happiness. We pushed past the cash desk and on towards the steps, and then I saw the poster. It was identical to the posters which had adorned the Kemble foyer all week, or almost identical. There were three differences and each one was a killer. It said:

MUSICAL MARIE
GAUMONT THEATRE WORCESTER
WILL ATTEMPT TO BREAK
THE WORLD RECORD FOR
NON-STOP PIANO PLAYING
123 HOURS.
MAY 17–22

I stopped and looked at Sid; he stopped and looked at me. We stood there dumb in the pressing crowd. Marie was a professional. In the time it took to read the poster, the whole fabric I'd so lovingly constructed fell round me in cold ruin. I stared and stared. The crowds were still struggling happily out and I felt desolated.

And then desolation receded. It was even shocking the way the resentment and bitterness simply flowed away. I searched for something nasty to amputate any growth of guilt.

'What a job! A public shitter!'

'To music!'

'Turds and music by courtesy of the Kemble!'

We laughed more than the childish crappery deserved. While we were extravagantly mocking another poster outside the theatre, two sawdust balls hit us in the back.

﷼ The Vigzol Oil Man

One month before my fourteenth birthday, Bill's Ford V8 Pilot, taking us to London for a fortnight's holiday, was in collision with a Vigzol oil van, on the A40 between Cheltenham and Northleach. Les was driving and would bring back the car that night; I sat between him and Mother. Gran Halley had come for the ride, and we had brought Phyllis, our neighbour, to keep her company on the return trip; they were both in the back. It was a grey August morning of drizzle and greasy roads but the journey had been uneventful until the driver of the van cut a corner and found himself swung into a skid by the slopping oil behind him and the black Ford Pilot directly in his path. Only Les saw him coming head-on, and braked hard, near-side wheels against the verge, which may have saved lives; we were certainly lucky that Gran Halley had wanted to come, for otherwise we would have been in Les's own flimsy Morris 8.

I knew nothing of the actual collision. I was reading a book, head down. The sharp braking pushed my face into the bakelite dashboard which shattered almost immediately under impact while, for good measure, I was thrown up against the windscreen. Anybody stunned in a crash seems to recall the vivid silence immediately following and then the slow dreamlike way in which events pick up the broken momentum. I looked round to see Gran on the floor of the car and then became aware I was bleeding. Mother feared danger through fire and helped me out, then Phyllis. Gran was sat upright on the seat but would not move, and we thought Les was dead, head back over his seat. The three of us slumped down on the verge at the side of the road; it was all very coolly done.

The driver of the oil van was shocked and limping towards us as we slowly sorted ourselves out, and very soon other motorists were stopping and doing what they could. The lorry drivers in particular were tremendous, marshalling traffic round the wrecks and bringing a variety of first-aid kits for my torn face. I was shocked into a deep calm, aware of my injuries but without any feeling. Gran Halley had cracked a rib and cut her gums. Somebody passed her a flask of brandy, and her sharp need for a good drink, and the keen smarting as the spirit hit her cut mouth, was a triumph of determination over experience. I took in the scene quietly and calmly, pressing a flannel to my wounds which would gather twenty-five stitches later that morning, and another two hundred in the subsequent plastic surgery hospital. I felt very serene and very brave—I didn't often have such an audience to play to, nor such a drama to have a part in. Somebody left to phone for help from Northleach, four miles away, and we settled down to wait for police and ambulance; it was a long wait as it turned out— half an hour.

Mother had begun her tirade against the Vigzol oil man as soon as he had limped to sit beside us, and went on non-stop until the ambulances arrived. There was no doubt it was his fault: the van and the Ford were head-on hard against the car's near-side verge. He had only one minor injury and it might have been better for him if he had been worse hurt. He might have escaped the fury of my mother's tongue as she lashed out at him, shocked at what had happened to her son, her husband and her grandmother. The man's leg was gashed just below his left knee; it was an odd injury—hardly any bleeding, and one layer of flesh cleanly cut to reveal yet another beneath it, un- broken, almost as if inside the outer leg another identical limb lay in waiting. He was a youngish, chubby man, desperately sorry for his loss of control over the van, punctuating Mother's accusations and condemnations with occasional attempts to explain what had happened, and shaking his head anxiously

from side to side. He said he could feel no pain in his leg and
that was one of his first mistakes, for Mother forced him to take
a look at Gran, moaning, still in the car—*she* was in pain: he
could count himself lucky. She made him look closely at her
son's face which was ruined for ever (thanks, Mum) and her
husband dead on the grass; she called out to Phyllis to number
her bruises and discomforts; she forced him to take in her
own torn clothes and the wreck of her father's car—all the result
of his lack of concentration and control. Phyllis, the innocent
friend, out for the day, and now look. Look. Look. Just look!
And always the mild face shook from side to side, accepting
blame, promising atonement, desperate for sympathy but in a
situation where he was quite alone and no sympathy would
come.

I felt embarrassment more than anything else and tried to
get Mother to stop, but she was a tigress whose cub had been
attacked and she was merciless. I don't think, in her anxiety
for us and her shock, she even stopped for breath. Even when
Les began to come round, to general relief, she never left her
victim's side or even faltered in the attack. When Gran was
finally eased from the car to join us, it was more fuel to her
fire: Gran was eighty—how could that age sustain what his
carelessness had brought upon her? She vowed retribution,
threatened prosecution, said people like him ought not to be
allowed on the roads. I thought her last accusation was
definitely weak in contrast to some of the magnificence which
had gone before, but I admired and loved her deeply at that
moment, for she was like some Trojan woman, after Troy, with
nothing left but the sheer unfairness of it all. Over her vituper-
ation, though, I felt a mixture of shame and fatigue; the feeling
that it was vaguely unsporting moved across my mind. For I
felt strongly that the driver who, in one moment of carelessness,
had caused all this was, after all, a victim too; and I was glad
when the Cheltenham and Northleach ambulances arrived to
bear us to our various hospitals.

I remember a great deal about the morning of the accident,
from the moment I looked round in the silent car to see Gran on

the floor until I stood up too suddenly to walk to the ambulance and felt very weak and sick. Various details have disappeared from mind, but I recall with alarming clarity the gash in the oil man's leg and every part of his clothes and features—I should recognize him tomorrow—as he shook his desperate head from side to side, being sorry sorry sorry, as my Trojan mother, pale with shock and worry, make-up smudged and lipstick smeared, tried to lift the burden from her own bruised shoulders and drop it on to his.

Apples and Tea

We begin with an image. Visualize at time of war a patrol moving into long-lost territory to recapture some distant settlement. The patrol sets out confidently enough, but then comes across subtle traps, neat ambushes. At certain points tempting paths lead away from the line of march. The journey is a struggle. Behold, at last, the settlement. But what of the tattered remnants of our patrol? How much are they still capable of recapturing? Half? Three-quarters? Probably less.

And that's how I see memory. Guilts from the past set out the obstacles; successes and joys lay down the decoys. We gather at best 75 per cent of the thing as it really happened and I can see why: most of the memorable happenings that inflict us are sad, so our defences work overtime to soften the recollections. The phrase 'down Memory Lane', for instance. The image here is roses, roses all the way with never a false trail in sight. Memory Lane goes nowhere—has nowhere it can go; if it has any point at all it lies in pointless wandering, but the cliché softens the fact and smooths away the sharp edges.

Not for me, however. If I blunder into that hazy tunnel in search of particular times of my life, I'm in for dark stumbling of doubt and deception, with absolute lack of certainty that, even if I find them, they'll look anything like they did the first time round. So we have to be careful with memory. Here are a few hard facts.

I was fourteen. I lived with the family in the big pub opposite the bus station. It was a Monday night and it was not yet nine.

This I know for sure: Monday night was darts night, when I filled in for any of the team failing to appear; it was considered convenient that I be told before nine if I had to play. I was doing my Latin prep, and I was doing it in the kitchen. I never understood—and never will—the point of Latin, and I was poor at it, so every night was Latin night. What makes it certain that I was involved with this exacting nonsense at the special time I'm writing of was that on Mondays I began my two hours of prep with the stuff, so I should be free to be called to the bar; other nights I left it till last. You can see how I'm trying to whip memory into line. It must have been winter, since I worked in my bedroom when the weather was warm, and working in the kitchen also meant that Harry, the Drifters' captain, knew where to find me at a moment's notice.

That's all I can promise as certain; you can rely on the story so far. The rest is subject to any distortion wicked enough to stir as I drag the subject by, but I'm trying. Here's something else: when the steps clacked up the passage to the kitchen door I thought it must be Harry or Doug Phillips. I also thought it must be nine and pushed the books aside waiting for the chirpy knocking at the door. Instead it was Nan who came in, hiding a hovering figure behind her.

'Have you got a moment to help this gentleman, love? Won't take you long. Make him a cup of tea: he'll explain.'

She shoved him in and introduced him. Significantly I can't remember his name; I shall call him Sowter. He hovered uneasily.

'Well now, boy. Your gran have told me of you.'

Mr. Sowter was one of our farming customers and very much the local type; red of face, clear of eye, massively wrinkled and very dark of tooth. He was in a suit. (That made the visit formal: someone was in for a request.) He was nervous, too, but I was an attractively arrogant kid and I don't suppose my curious scrutiny helped as he continued to hover over me. Suddenly he dived into a pocket and brought out four apples which he laid carefully on the table—gnarled, warty, scaly and green: freaks. He saw my reaction, and I took pity.

'Thanks, Mr. Sowter. Thanks a lot. Nan said you'd like a cup of tea.'

'Right good on her, young man.'

Right good on her. I noted the syntax as a fact of life, neither good nor bad, just interesting.

'Well, Nan said for you to have a cup.' I filled the kettle and set it on the gas. I talked like that at home, anyway. School was different. I mention this syntax and turn of speech because it's soon to play something of a part. 'What was it you wanted me to do, Mr. Sowter?'

He carefully put down his cup and leaned forward across the table.

'She be in Birmin-ham, my boy. Middle on the night they took her from the house last week. Middle on the night, mind.' He was impressed with his drama. 'First to the County Hospital over on beyond the buses; then they have took her to Birmin-ham hospital, my boy. And that where she be now.'

He leaned back to see the effect on me. I guessed he'd been talking of his wife and said I was sorry. Forward he came again.

'I know as you be sorry. And your gran now, she did say, "Mr. Sowter", she did say, "You see my grandson out in the kitchen. You needs a scholar." So she brung me to you. I told her how you should have happles.'

Mr. Sowter had need of a scholar! I tried not to grin but not hard enough. He saw, and held up his right hand. It was a mess: red, swollen; the centre knuckles thrust up like ugly marbles, bruised. I stopped grinning.

'Damn tractor handle done it, boy. Kick back, her did. Damn nuisance, boy.'

I nodded back. God, it was a mess. He examined it carefully. I wished he'd put it back in his pocket.

'But no writing, young man, no, none. Does you see it now, son? I hopes as how she may be comin' home the other side on a week or two, but her must have letters, young man. Damn it, her must.'

This then was the request. He shoved his wounded hand into

a pocket, and it hurt him. 'Damn and how I forgets it now and then! Wait you one minute.'

Delicately the hand was withdrawn, and in it lay a scrap of paper which he passed over. I smoothed it out: the address of a particular hospital in Birmingham.

'Her must have letters, son. And you do have enough of paper!'

He was right there: not writing paper, however. I told him to wait while I fetched some, but he said, 'Damn no. That be paper, ain't him?'

(Which was in some sense symptomatic of any number of earlier difficulties I'd faced. English Text Book, say, page 200, exercise Six, sentence number Four. 'Parse and comment on the following:"Damn no. That be paper, ain't him?"') I pulled my Latin exercise book towards me and opened it at the centre. I set to. We began.

I can report I managed well enough with the address of the Sowter farm which was beautiful and deeply rural, in Marcle or Orcop, or Pixley, or somewhere similar. But the problem was not in the words: the accent was thick and aromatic, like pipe smoke—I could grab them through it. The problem was in the syntax, the grouping. For God's sake, what did it mean? Exactly mean?

'And I do hope as how you be comin' good enough.' I don't promise that's entirely genuine but I'll swear it's no more than a couple of points off verbatim. I copied it down, read it back (feeling my accent broadening to his). I wrote every word he offered, trusting it would hold some real meaning to Mrs. Sowter.

'. . . and I do trust, my dear, as how they be well caring of you . . .' So long as I remembered the grouping of the words it sounded passable and Sowter nodded as I read it back. But it looked terrible.

Anyway, in such vein Mr. Sowter trusted that his lady was being fed regularly and well; he promised her eggs when he visited her—though she might well be home too soon for a visit. Love was sent not only by him but by a nightmare host of relatives and friends who had every name, I swear, in Genesis, and whose spelling stretched my narrow biblical knowledge to its limit.

Then we closed: 'My own dear wife—I do miss you and the old house don't seem right.' That caught me; I thought it was very sad.

I came to the end of my task. 'Do I sign your name for you?'

He laughed. 'Damn no. We shall do well. Give us the pen, young man.' Laborious and brave with his painful hand, he scrawled a heavy signature.

I looked at it hard. 'I can't read it.'

He laughed again, more quietly. 'But her shall read it, son, and know.'

Then he suddenly stood; he'd brought an old coat with him. 'You be busy, young man. I can see.'

I helped him gingerly on with his coat and wished his hand speedy recovery for which he thanked me. He looked speculatively at his ruined fist. 'All in the hands of Him as knows.'

I opened the door; he turned in the passage. 'You shall have happles if and so we shall send another.'

I looked at the freaks and tried to look enthusiastic. He walked heavily away, towards the bars. I called after him, above the noise: 'I'll get some proper paper.' But he didn't look back.

I moved, whistling, back to the table and began gathering up the cups and saucers. I truly hoped he would come again. He'd interrupted my Latin—I knew I'd never finish it properly now. He'd used two pages of my Latin exercise book but with luck George, the master, would be too boozed to notice, and it seemed as if I'd have to supply a stamp as well as an envelope, but I hoped he'd come again. For among the quiet sincerity of his hopelessly jumbled words, I was beginning to find a relevant statement forming. Latin was being put in its place, for a start. What did it matter that the object must always go into the accusative? What matter dative, gerunds, kings and sailors who were always carrying spears, queens who sang sweet songs eternally to boys who were good (and occasionally gave them apples!), supines, superlatives, infinitives, deponents? What

were this whole manic horde of nothingness compared to
Mr. Sowter whose hand was hurt, whose apples were awful,
whose own dear wife was sick, alone in Birmingham, and whose
house, in that poignant sentence, just didn't seem right? It was
one of the saddest statements I had ever heard.

Nan came in to find out what he'd wanted. She rolled the
apples over distastefully and we grinned.

The following Monday, at the same time, in the same suit,
Sowter came again. His hovering awkwardness was the same,
too. We both felt it, and acted.

'Happles, my boy.'

'Cup of tea. Kettle's on.'

And I began to understand something about ritual: he
polished the freaks and I set up tea. Tea and apples became
wholly necessary and entirely unimportant. Meanwhile, we
grew used to each other again beneath their camouflage.

But there was a difference. He held out a letter. 'Mrs. Sowter
have sent us a letter.' He pushed it proudly across the table.

'How is she then? Better?'

'In the hands of Him as knows.' He sat back expectantly.

I didn't at first understand. 'You want me to read it?'

He nodded. I was not happy.

'But it's private, isn't it?'

'Damn, boy, and how shall I know when you don't read him
for me.'

I was still not happy. He leaned forward and tapped the
table with his good hand. 'Damn, boy, and how shall I read
him when the glasses be bust!'

I still didn't like it, but I took out the letter and read: 'My
dear husband, Very many thanks for your kind letter which I
received safely today. I am very glad to hear your news. I am
very glad you are managing to keep the farm running
smoothly . . ."'

Sowter nodded, frowned, smiled at more or less the appropriate places at the news from Lady Grenfell Ward in that
Birmingham hospital, but I was far from easy. It was not the
privacy of the letter that disturbed me, and it was not the

contents—there was, after all, just a single page (but we had
sent four); it was rather the *lack* of personality. The page began
as I've said and continued with such facts as the necessity for
further tests, the advisability of a minor exploratory operation,
the general comfort and well-being of Mrs. Sowter and, last,
the hurling back of greetings into that rout from Genesis.

The letter closed: '. . . Looking forward to seeing you soon.
Please write again. All my love. Kath.' As I read this out
Sowter's eyes filled with tears, and I was moved at his emotion.
I left him to it.

'I'll clear up. Then we'll write back.'

I took out the tray and spent extra minutes washing up the
few cups and saucers. I needed to think. 'Very many thanks'?
'Please write again'? What sort of exchange was stiff, impartial
speech like that for 'I do miss you and the old house don't seem
right'? And the writing—as neat and efficiently antiseptic as,
doubtless, Lady Grenfell Ward itself. I hadn't of course seen
Sowter's own handwriting but I was willing to bet it couldn't
match the small, petty roundness of his wife's, and this made
me sad. My writing, however, was better than either's—I
flaunted it at every opportunity; it was beautiful but with a
definite personality—and I resolved there and then to capture
every slight quirk of Sowter's speech and preserve it in the
amber of my pure calligraphy.

Purpose shone through me as I poised my pen at the table
for our reply. Sowter began: 'My own dear wife, my dear.
Very joyed of having your loving letter.'

Well done, Sowter! I wielded my pen, then read it back:
'. . . "of having your loving letter." '

'I shall come to Birmin-ham, sure, and you shall have eggs
from our old house. Who should come to the house today, my
dear, but Ben and Jacob . . .'

And so on, much as before. More ranks of biblical characters
filled the page; there was news of stock, crops, of markets and
disease. Down it went—every last word. I had a mission, a task
not without nobility. If I'd had time I would have felt rather
smug.

Of course, I met the occasional difficulty: 'Have I got this right, Mr. Sowter? . . . "Barley up the high ten acre don't stand well for the month"?'

And Sowter would suddenly look at me, bemused by the apparent stupidity of the question, and nod.

'Sorry, Mr. Sowter.'

He closed: 'My own dear wife—you must write again for we all do miss you. Old Bruce do pine bad.' He always got me in the last sentence.

The signature was made with difficulty, though I thought the hand much improved. I could still not decipher it: it appeared to begin with H. Sowter rose. I helped him into his coat.

'Young man, I do thank you. For the letter and the tea.'

Then he turned and walked to the bars, and that was that. He didn't notice the brand-new paper and envelopes I'd bought for him; he made no mention of stamps. He couldn't actually know, of course, that I'd had to spend the whole of my morning, lunch and afternoon breaks clearing George's Latin out of the way to save the time for him.

I called down the passage, 'See you next week, I suppose.' He walked on, raised a hand. 'Thanks for the lovely happles!'

I could be a nasty little sod when I wanted. But he should at least have noticed the paper. I closed the kitchen door; sarcasm was simply beyond Sowter's experience.

I sat at the table and reflected further, intrigued at this letter from his wife. It made sense: I must have heard the story a dozen times before. Well-to-do farmer's daughter, superior, rolled in the hay by one of her dad's lowly farm workers. Result: educated woman, often of great resolution and intelligence, harnessed for life to well-meaning, slow, simple husband. Big farmerdaddy puts them into a farm, not too near his own, and both families pretend it would have happened anyway. Everyone makes the best of it. It made me sadder still, and I found that Sowter—simple, friendly Sowter—was beginning to take on certain heroic qualities. I saw him as the mainstay of his farm, his wife practical but distant. I saw him longing for just one day, perhaps, in the autumn of their lives—late autumn, it

D

would have to be now—when he and the farmer's bitter daughter might meet on some real level of warm, affectionate communication.

Meanwhile Old Bruce do pine bad. Yet she, callous bitch, could only reprove his warm, natural tongue—Sowter's, I mean—with a certain cool surprise that he was managing to run the farm without her. I was a sensitive kid and could raise my own emotional temperature not only with ease but with a certain melancholic pleasure. I ground my teeth for my old friend and the pining Bruce, and when Harry put his head round the door to ask me to partner Doug Burgoyne I was in the right mood. God help the opposition!

And so came Sowter for six or seven weeks with never a Monday missed.

There were more changes. It must have been her third letter: '. . . I am feeling very poorly as a result of the tests but the doctor assures me it is for the best and everyone remains very kind. . . .' More changes. '. . . Please come and visit me soon. . . .'

This was important. I looked hard at Sowter who shifted uneasily. 'You said you were going last week.'

He looked away. 'Damn, boy, and how can I go visit to Birmin-ham! Look on that hand, boy!'

It was almost back to normal.

'That damn old tractor; she right done for me. Damn and who must do the work when I goes off to Birmin-ham?'

He was shifty and kept his eyes from mine; he was scared. People like Sowter do well enough in their own context—I'd found out his context was a small, rather run-down farm—but force him into Birmingham's Bull Ring, subject to strangers, and I could see he might be scared enough to deny his wife her visit. Still, we pressed on . . .

'And we hopes as how you must soon be home. Like you said—'

'Two weeks ago.'

'. . . Like you said—'

'Before the tests.'

He laid his hand on the table, feebly. 'That old tractor . . .'

That was the first disillusionment; the second followed within a week or two. The boring sequence of the two taps on the door, the awkward hovering, the apples, the coat, the tea; we ran through the ritual. He sat down, beginning to be a nuisance. I waited for him to produce the Birmingham letter.

'Damn, boy. I do know as I got him somewheres!'

'No hurry.'

It was somewhere, but where? Not that I was particularly interested. I tapped my pen idly on the table and whistled to myself as he rummaged through his pockets and laid the detritus before him—matches, wallet, spectacles. The spectacles that were supposed to be smashed. I stopped whistling.

'Damn and he be here somewheres!' Then he forced that supposedly tender and useless hand, with no wince or recoil, into a small waistcoat pocket and tugged the letter out.

He caught my glance and dithered. It was no real surprise: I'd suspected for a week or two that Sowter could neither read nor write. At the moment of truth, when he knew that I knew, we both ran for cover.

'I have brought you happles, my boy.'

'Tea's almost ready.'

He polished. I prepared. I called to him, 'Your hand still looks bad.'

'Damn, boy, and you be right.'

'Mrs. Sowter writes very small.'

'She do, boy. Too small for my old eyes.'

Well, it would do. It didn't much matter—except that the heroic Sowter was shrinking again. I poured the tea. I didn't care a damn if he were or were not illiterate. In fact, I could have admired a blunt admission: 'My boy, I can neither read nor write!' Very Rousseau, very Wordsworth; I'd have liked that. But all this sneaky excuse-making, and the shiftiness, the shame. Sowter, then became less ideal, less worth slaving for. A real nuisance. I acted accordingly.

He dictated: 'And you knows, my dear wife, as how it be none easy spreading over on that corner six-acre. . . .' And I wrote: 'The small corner field is difficult to fertilize.'

'Okay. Got it. Next.'

And so on. Looking back, it seems a silly revenge but he'd let me down badly. The noble savage who had sought youthful aid with dignity and gratitude was fast becoming a feeble yokel too scared to stray from his cabbage patch, unwilling to risk shaming himself in the eyes of a fourteen-year-old kid who couldn't have cared less, and one who was demanding an hour of my time each and every week.

'So my loving wife, do take great care now. Lone work be poor at sunset . . .' Now that was too much; I suspected he did it deliberately. I wrote: 'Look after yourself. Missing you.'

'Okay. Go on.'

'Your own very loving husband . . .' I wrote, 'Yours sincerely.'

'Okay. Sign.'

If only he'd *admit* it . . . I didn't *want* him to shrink. When I chose a hero I insisted he proved me right.

'Now then, my boy. Next Monday.'

'All right.'

Then the final tedious putting on of the coat, shutting of the door, shuffling up the passage—and me left behind with work to do and the tea things to clear away, let down.

I suppose I must have written about eight letters in all and was waiting for Sowter to disgorge number nine. We were back to paper from an exercise book—though not George's—and Nan was briefed to get some stamp money from him afterwards. Perhaps I could say I had to go back to school on Monday evenings: he'd not know differently. But what about the darts?

I was, as you see, in no very good mood when I heard him in the passage, but maybe she would have stuck in something juicy about the piddling little op she'd just had. The steps shuffled closer and the door was tapped, opened. I sighed and pushed the Latin away, saying to myself in a thick grotesque parody of his accent, 'I have brung you happles, my buoy!'

But his eyes were red. His mouth motioned but gave no sound. He drew out four apples and laid them softly on the table. Round his arm he wore a black band. He looked at me and his eyes filled. He closed the door behind him.

Time thickened to nothing; I heard Harry outside. 'Eyup, Sowter. Finished with him, have you?' And then a jaunty tap brought him in. 'Eyup, Professor. We're short again. Fancy partnering Phil?'

I could make no reply. He stared at me unhappily. 'What's up, son?'

What was up was that Mrs. Sowter was dead but I made no reply. Harry retreated to bring reinforcements but Mrs. Sowter was dead. I tried not to feel involved, guilty for the skeleton letters I'd sent. Tried not to feel bad about Sowter and the way I'd put him down so badly. But nothing helped. Nan came with Harry and Phil, but nothing helped. I never saw Sowter again and even forgot him in a month or two.

The weather turned and spring breezed in; I took to doing my prep. in my light room at the top of the house. I fought with Latin and thought of girls; I read Xenophon and thought of girls. I even thought of girls while I was wrestling with logarithms and you can have no more poignant symptom of spring fever than that.

I don't know what day it was, or even what time, but sometime in spring when Sowter was forgotten and I was thinking of girls, Nan climbed the two flights of stairs to call me down to the bar. 'Busy?'

With Xenophon? She had to be joking.

'Come down to the bar then. Someone there who wants to meet you!'

To meet me. Me? I could tell by Nan's grin it was a girl. God Almighty!

'I'll just do my hair.'

'She's having a drink with Don; there's only the three of us.'

My God, it was better than a girl: it was a woman. Maybe even a girlish woman which was best of all. I did wonders in two minutes and scrutinized the mirror for spots. No. Good.

When I saw her I was only mildly disappointed. I wildly desired older women and she was at the most twenty-five; maybe she was even twenty-two. Or twenty.

'This is Miss Hopcroft.'

'How do you do.' I was smarmy. She smiled.

'Hello.'

Nan moved behind the counter to serve Don.

'Miss Hopcroft is a nurse.'

'I used to work in Birmingham.'

All right. You know what's going to happen; how it's all going to tie neatly up. But you've been only very slightly involved, if at all. You've probably been able to spot the last possible piece of a possible pattern. Good for you. Remember: I was only fourteen, and I couldn't. To you it's possibly corn; to me . . . I've never really found out.

'Remember the Sowters?' Miss Hopcroft said. 'Remember Mrs. Sowter?'

I remembered.

'Well, I helped nurse her. I worked on Lady Grenfell Ward. We were great buddies, poor old thing.' Miss Hopcroft had light tinkling laughter. 'I heard so much about Hereford—the farm and this place, and you. I thought I just had to drop in whenever I was near enough.'

Miss Hopcroft was on holiday. Nan poured her a drink.

'You and your grandson could do no wrong, according to our Harold!'

Harold! I'd guessed Herbert—and a sudden shock possibility heaved into sight. 'He visited her?'

'What? I should say so!' Again the tinkling laughter.

Sowter had visited her!

'Our Harold came to see us two or three times in his brown baggy suit and big black boots! Laugh! Did he ever unload his horrible old apples on you?'

I was going off Miss Hopcroft. To my horror, Nan joined in. 'Happles, you mean!'

'That's right. Happles!' They laughed together.

'Birmin-ham!'

'Yes. I'd forgotten that one!'

I didn't laugh. Somewhere a tide was beginning to turn. Somewhere a heroic Sowter was raising his golden shield. How dare they? He'd made himself go, forced himself; maybe it was even me that had driven him there. How dare they mock him? I felt dangerous.

Miss Hopcroft was enjoying herself. 'You say you never met the wife? She was just as you'd imagine. Small and wiry.'

I'd thought so.

'Very upright and sharp.'

I'd thought so.

'And just like him: couldn't read or write a word!'

I sat very still. I said, 'Sorry? *She* couldn't? Or *he* couldn't?'

'She couldn't. I had to read his letters to her and then she used to tell me what she wanted to say in reply and I wrote back. She was very ill, of course. I could hardly make out a word she said, what with the accent and the way she put it all. I just used to stick down what I imagined to be the general gist! Now you know why your grandmother thought we just had to meet!'

She laughed. Nan laughed. Don had been listening and he laughed too.

'I used to look over our Harold and wonder how his writing could be so good!'

The bar rang with the clamour of their laughing. I sat very very still, dangerous.

'So you and me, we wrote to each other for a couple of months! Don't you think it's hilarious?'

'Excuse me.' I stepped delicately to the door and closed it quietly behind me.

Didn't I think it hilarious. I don't much want to analyse now what I think was happening to me then: presumably it would be impossible anyway. But the whole business was somehow a milestone.

As I said at the beginning, we remember what we want to remember. If events or words or names have come out wrongly the feelings—such as I've been able to identify—are accurate. I feel confident of that. I'm sure I remember what I felt.

I remember, for instance, that, back in my room, I began to cry. Then suddenly felt too sad for that. I remember thinking that was odd. I suppose it was because I'd stopped thinking of

Sowter and was now more concerned with that bloody woman downstairs. The image of Sowter in Lady Grenfell Ward with his desperate apples as peace-tokens to all who would take them was pitiful—I could cry for that. But what had wiped that picture clean away was nothing more than my pure anger at her mocking him, having written letters like that, having expected me to join the laughter too.

Finally, I began to laugh. Giggle would perhaps be the better word. And the final benefit of several from the long, miserable adventure made itself known. I realized I was a giggling idiot because, somewhere inside me, something infinitely smart preferred me giggling and not guilty or upset. As a sort of useful rider, I swallowed, with no effort or surprise, the fact that this particular mess of emotions had been stirred up by a young and attractive woman.

So, I cleaned myself up and did my hair again. I made the habitual spot-check and left the room. I'd make for the laughter, I'd sit close to this woman. And I'd smile and smile and smile.

I think I learned more from apples and tea than ever I did from Latin.

A Snapshot Album of My Father

1940?—HEREFORD

1. Young child in pram
The baby gapes as giants heave by and the pram rocks over
cobbles. The image has a brittle quality, thin. One certainty:
the giant pushing his pram is his father and one eye is funny.

(His mother once said: 'He used to leave his glass eye lying
about; when he was drunk he'd stick it in upside down—he
knew I hated it.')

1942—PLYMOUTH

1. Wartime train
Of the long wartime train journey the child remembers only
darkness, noise, sickness. The corridors are full of soldiers and
sailors, and in the eerie excitement of the Severn tunnel tons of
water press on ears as the train roars under.

2. Plymouth, after blitz
Plymouth smoulders on a grey day. Rubble is in the streets
and people walk slowly. The mother drags the child to visit its
father. The child will see a face, a figure in a uniform, but no
more of the visit will register because—

3. Fish stall
because suddenly—NOW—the one vivid memory to fix in absolute clarity while the mother hauls her son through the smoking

streets—NOW—there is a fish stall and the counter is crawling with the slow snapping and creeping of crabs; the surface is a slow shifting of grotesque shells that clack and scrape as they scrabble over each other to pile at the counter's raised edge where there is nowhere left to crawl. The child has never seen anything like these creatures and he is transfixed, too scared to scream.

(His mother once said: 'He never sent us any maintenance after the first few months.')

1942—EXETER

1. Grandma and Grandpa Rowe
The mother and child visit her husband's parents above the bank in Exeter. Grandma Rowe is thin and snappy but Grandpa Rowe gives the child half a crown and likes jam on his porridge. The child wonders what Nan and Bill are doing at home, feels unnecessary, a burden.

2. The back staircase
But the back staircase behind the bank is a delight. The stairs are marble and concrete, speckled, clean, with a swoony smell. The echoes are thunder. Sometimes he secretly licks the clean marble stairs and when he dares to look out over Exeter from the tiny precise window at the turning near the top he is flying.

(His mother once said: 'The Rowes think the sun shines from their backsides.')

1943—HEREFORD

1. The Commercial: cellar
The boy's father is coming to see his wife and child, on leave. Everybody tries so hard to get him excited that he guesses it's not compulsory. He is playing with clay pipes in the cellar when his father clatters down, grinning, in uniform, with presents from Egypt. A strange box, battered and black, is full of coins and cards, buttons and badges, and there is a camel

whip, curling, with a strange smell. The boy pounds up to the kitchen to show Nan, Bill and Mum.

2. *The Commercial: pantry*

The boy's father leaves secretly behind, for his son's Christmas present, a complete set of real oilskins, teenage size, but since the boy has years to go yet and Hereford sees no sea storms, they will never be worn. They lie forgotten beneath the long table in the pantry so long that the oil seeps down through the folded skins and they are eventually removed to the dustbin, a hard, sticky, tar-smelling pack.

(His mother often said: 'He never had a penny but he'd act like Lord Muck.')

1943—HEREFORD

1. *The Commercial: sick child upstairs*

The boy lies sick with measles in his mother's dark room where a bed has been made up. He has a temperature and is toying with the fantasy that recurs each time his blood heats this way: the walls of the room swell, press and fold round him. He watches intently for he can make them move, make them stop—sometimes—by grinding teeth and groaning so that the blood rushes noisily round his head until it hurts. Then he stops and begins to fall asleep seeing, finally, the walls slip back smoothly to safe proportions.

Waking delicately, probing towards better health, the boy reaches for the handkerchief beneath his pillow. It takes time: it will hurt if he lifts his head to find it. But at last fingers close on a corner of linen and drag it carefully to his nose and he blows slowly, to prevent head aching.

'We don't do that, son.'

The boy is confused to have the father easing the corner of his bed's top sheet from his nose. His father produces a handkerchief of his own and closes the boy's fingers round it, holding fingers and nose, insisting on a proper blow. It is humiliation: his father believes he is the sort of little boy who snots on his sheet. The smell of the man's handkerchief almost makes the boy sick.

(His mother said: 'He only comes back when he's run out of money.')

1943—HEREFORD

1. The Commercial: kitchen

The boy is absorbed by an enormous brown paper bag of marbles his father has brought. He already has marbles but these are bigger, of clear glass with nuggets of bright colour inside—you can look right through them. His father has come from Plymouth with Uncle Jim. It is the profusion of marbles that impresses the boy; there must be a hundred. He counts them, he rolls them and occasionally flicks them, but there is nobody to show off to in the kitchen and he has been told not to go into the bars. The grownups have all gone to the down-stairs lounge. He balances a marble on each eye, head flat back, and tries to open his eye lids but his mother comes to take him by the shoulders.

'When they say who do you want to go with, you say me.'

2. The Commercial: downstairs lounge

In the lounge all his grownups are sitting without drinks. His mother is there, and Nan and Bill; his father is there, too, with the stranger Uncle Jim. Something is happening; there are no drinks and nobody is laughing. His father comes to him, smiling, and crouches down to be the same size—the boy would prefer to be picked up and be the same size as him. It is something about father living in Plymouth while mother lives here at the Commercial and who does he want to go with. The boy is obedient and says he wants to go with his mother. His father stands up and the boy has the sense of having been important because nothing else is said and no one moves for a long time. The question, in any case, makes no sense—unthinkable, literally, to be anywhere else but here, at home, with Mother, Nan, Bill, Thelma, Harry and Phil. He hopes his father will let him keep the marbles.

(His mother said: 'If he'd cared anything for us he wouldn't have gone away in the first place.')

1947—DEVON

1. Children playing in a fish market
The fishmarket smell is new to the boy; they do not have it in Hereford and he hates it. He chases with his cousins over wet cobbles on his first holiday outside Herefordshire alone. He is staying with his father but spends most of the time with his cousins who are older. He likes them.

2. The sea
The boy stares out to sea. They do not have sea in Hereford. He tries to assess the limitations of the water and visualize the foreign shore on which it must crash, or the alien sea with which it must merge. The cousins hover and mope: they have grown up with the sea and do not understand the problems it is posing to their visitor.

3. Street corner
The house where he stays is on a corner and the boy walks there with his girl cousin. Two boys of her age approach and she whispers to be careful. The pairs close. The boy is timid, on the edge of panic: he knows if it comes to action he will let her down, and Father, Mother and all Hereford. The pairs draw level; the boys jeer and the girl snaps back. Then suddenly the danger is past and the boys laugh as they dawdle away. One turns, grinning, warning the boy to be careful. The girl pulls him into the safe door and says to take no notice.

4. Attic
The semi-darkness of the attic is another novelty and delights the boy with its dusty bric-à-brac and secrecy. He peers from the grimy window on the wet streets as his cousin stretches on an old bed and softly asks if he wants to see her operation scar. The boy does not know what to say and gazes down from the window, trying to locate the direction the two boys have taken,

but he is called to the bed and asked again. His cousin is stretched out, skirt to her chest and blue knickers held down at one point for the boy to see the scar on her tummy. She tells him to feel it, which he does, shrinking from the idea, but she takes his hand and presses his negative fingertips against the puckered line of tissue and further down where she lets his hand go free. He has the familiar sense of being extra, redundant. Dumb with doubt, he stands by the dusty bed with his dead hand thrust inside the knickers. He already knows a handful of dirty pub songs and has a hazy notion of sex but none of it squares with this girl cousin in a secret attic in wet, alien Devon where he is visiting his father after the divorce.

(His mother once said: 'They'll do anything to hold on to you if you go down there.')

1948—HEREFORD
Two pictures from another album.

1. The Booth Hall: bride, groom and son
The oak-panelled dining hall of the Booth is packed with family and friends. The boy's mother looks young and pretty; Les is tall and shy, with bad teeth. The photographer sets up for a picture of bride and groom but the boy is called to complete the group.

He comes to stand between them and turns, smiling, to his stepfather. 'Hello, Dad.'

Sensation; the gathering breaks up, visibly moved. Great-aunts weep and strong men gulp. The timing is perfect. The emphasis shifts slyly from step-father to boy. As he intended.

2. The Booth Hall: bride's son and friend
Sid, his friend, and the boy—released early from school for the occasion—raise lemonade glasses to the photographer who snaps away, knowing when he's on to a good thing.

(Mother once said: 'The Rowes are full of bullshit but the Edwardses have got the money.')

1954—SWAINSHILL, HEREFORDSHIRE

1. The Kite's Nest: living room
The youth comes down from his room in his mother's and step-father's pub to meet his father and stepmother who are holiday-ing in Wales and have called at short notice. He has no idea of an appropriate response and decides on amiability. There is tea and sandwiches but the occasion is formal and awkward. Five grownups—if he counts himself which he does—held in an interesting web of relationships sit round the edge of the room and talk, when at all, of touring, Wales, good roads and the weather, as if any diversion from distant civility could lead suddenly to panic, revelation and guilt. The youth would like to know why his parents divorced; were they ever in love; how had they fared in separation; had they regrets. Instead he passes round plates and answers polite questions about school. Above all he would like to know why his father and mother married in the first place. Instead he holds open the front door and shakes hands as his father and stepmother pass through.

(His mother often said: 'I had to sell my engagement ring to buy you boots and don't forget it.')

1956—DEVON

1. Plymouth station
The train pulls in and the youth is surprised at the easy identi-fication of his father, who makes no reference to the youth's uniform—a cadet sergeant-major and smart with it—come to Plymouth for a course with 42 Commando. The Rowes are traditionally Navy. Betty, his stepmother, says how trim he looks.

2. Torquay illuminations
It is dark as they pass through Torquay on the way to the house in Newton Abbot. His father and Betty are proud of the illumin-ations so the youth hides indifference beneath a show of enthusiasm; after eighteen years of pub life he can act any emotion—the ease of it always shocks him.

3. Newton Abbot: 5 Station Road
The house is small and comfortable but the youth has to report
to barracks tomorrow and his father and Betty will drive him
back to Plymouth, visiting relatives on the way. Betty and his
father take care to steer away from difficult conversation and
the youth would feel happier if he were proving better company.
Ghosts are after him: he knows his mother hates his being here.
He wants to talk of the past, to explain the sheet and the
marbles, but it is impossible. At breakfast he lies about his bad
night's sleep and clumsily brings the subject round to blowing
his sick childhood nose on the corner of his sickbed sheet. His
father has no memory of this at all and the youth feels a flash of
relief and annoyance: all that guilt for nothing. As if it were
an answer—which, in view of the surrealism of the breakfast-
table conversation, maybe it is—his father recalls the youth's
childhood dislike of the daily morning duty of blowing his nose
on lavatory paper and the youth has absolutely no recollection
of this. He wonders if one event could have triggered different
memories, neither of which actually happened. The alternative
is ludicrous: the one retrospective mutual concern—blowing
noses.

4. Topsham, near Exeter: Uncle Ed's mink farm
Uncle Ed has a mink farm where he also keeps hens. A number
of the hens have one leg only. Uncle explains that the hens
insist upon flapping on to the top of the minks' cages where the
vicious little creatures snap at their limbs. The youth laughs at
this but both men look at him solemnly, finding no humour.
Uncle Ed had to destroy a hen who, one leg already bitten off,
had nevertheless lurched on to the wire roofing and had the
other taken too. The youth finds this very funny indeed and the
men shake their heads and grin at him.

5. Plymouth station again
The course is over and the father has come alone to see his son
back on to the train for Newport and Hereford. He sees the
youth off and they shake hands. As the train pulls out, he says,
'Keep your chin up.'

(His mother said: 'Typical of the Rowes to show off to you.')

1963—SWAINSHILL, HEREFORDSHIRE

1. The Kite's Nest: living room
The man hears of his father's death. It is a strange sensation to reach this unique moment and find that it fails to stir any great feelings. The man is less stirred at his father's painful progress towards death by cancer than by the way the news has arrived. For it is his first day home after the end of his university career: the final exams are all taken and he will travel back to Cambridge to learn results and collect the remaining luggage in a week or so. Betty has sent the letter, with firm instructions on the envelope that it is to await his arrival. She tells him that it was his father's wish that he should not be troubled with news of either sickness or death until his exams and post-exam celebrations were over. When the man tells his mother he is careful to observe her reactions and is hurt and relieved to find them as negative as his own.

2. The Kite's Nest: garden
In the garden, the man is approached by Les. 'Had a bit of bad news, I hear.'

Well yes, the baby/child/boy/youth/man has to agree. So much now impossible ever to know, with this death, which probably he would never have asked anyway. Too late for funeral or flowers. A shadowy area on the edges of his life will now be there for ever, to swell, fold and close in on him at times of heated blood and worse, and grinding teeth will no longer help.

(My mother often says: 'You're so like your father; I can see so much of him in you.')

E

The Dido of Stonebow Road

There are some people you can picture in such sharp focus that they can have no life in the memory beyond that; the image is perfect, self-contained, precluding addition or embroidery. Nellie Davies was like that. She obstinately refuses to be made into a story.

She was always nearly old and her voice rasped hoarsely. She always dressed in black and her sharp, sallow face with her straw-coloured hair was always crowned by a black straw hat with a hatpin. Nell lived in a little house very near the slaughter-house in Stonebow Road, not far from the Commercial, and was Jug & Bottle trade. This was more akin to Public Bar custom—that was where her husband, Skipper, drank—but was a tiny wood-panelled room with a separate entrance and one wooden chair which Nell took for her own. She drank Guinness and her aggressive South Wales nature frequently came out when she had had too much, or—as the Private Bar remarked—too little. When I was very small I used to draw her, unfairly, as a witch and scare myself by taking secret peeps at her sitting stately in the Jug & Bottle.

She worked, on and off for years, as a cleaner for Nan, always reliable up to a point, prim in her floral pinafore over the habitual black; but beyond that point something would happen, some word be carelessly said, and that was that until either we needed her badly again, or she needed us. At her best she was very conscientious and two habits distinguished her from Renée, our more permanent cleaner, who was reliable and easygoing;

both habits stemmed maybe from the fact that she had once been in service. First, Nell always wore a mask of a smile for those of us in the family (though not for Renée), which could explode into hostility if anyone upset her. Second, when I was taking my O levels and my room was a mess of books and papers, she dusted them over with a goose feather so she should not disturb their learned chaos. Sadly, she became more and more grossly polite to me as the 'professor' took over from the kid running wild round the bars.

Skipper, like his wife, seemed always to wear the same outfit; his was blue overalls and a flat cap, for he worked for the Council. He was a slight, quiet man, always smiling, with rosy cheeks and a pipe. He liked to plunge a red-hot poker into his cider to warm it when the weather was cold. He sat contentedly, one wall away from his voluble wife, and reminded me of a Popeye without the frenzy.

Nell, on the other hand, had a feeling for drama. If she were told anything even mildly surprising, her body would jar to a halt, in any position, and her mouth gape. 'Good Got!' she would say, her eyes two piercing beacons of absolute disbelief. Then, as you passed on, after the slightest pause, the scrubbing, polishing or whatever would continue and the throaty tuneless singing take up where you had broken into it, the shocking revelation heard, duly reacted to and forgotten, as per contract.

Her greatest performance was at Skipper's funeral. Whether the circumstances were simply so dramatic that they demanded a response, or whether out of some deep sense of real loss, Nell leapt suddenly into the open grave, crying, 'Bury me too!' and would not, for some time, allow herself to be talked out so that the sextons could fill Skipper in.

I listened enthralled when I was told the details; it was the nearest I had come to grand passion since I had heard *Aïda* in Rome on a school trip, and almost as fatuous. For weeks Nell was cherished by the sentimental Public Bar, a heroine on the grand scale. We were not used to such excess. Guinness was offered in large quantities, partly out of sympathy for Skipper's decease and partly in desperate propitiation lest she should release such dynamic feeling upon us again. She was a grieving widow for some time; it was a good strong part to play and it seemed as if she had always worn the weeds, just to be ready to catch the time.

But leaping like that down into the damp cleaving earth: I warmed to the magnificence of the gesture and did my share of handing over the stout. In the Private Bar where spirits were more cynical, they watched the votive offerings passing across the counter of the Jug & Bottle with stony faces and wondered if the plain fact hadn't been that Nell couldn't bear to see Skipper shunted into his eternal rest without walking all over him just one more time.

⧸ Totty Kear

Eight years old and will some good, kind grownup tell me what I'm doing adrift on this huge stage of Cheltenham Town Hall, goggling down at a sea of smiling teeth? I step forward and begin:

> *'How sad a thing it is to see*
> *Jam tarts for him but not for me.*
> *My heart is so unhappy, 'cause*
> *It wants some ginger beer through straws.*
> *Even a currant with a bun*
> *Would give me just a taste of fun.*
> *It's very hard to be so small—*
> *You don't get anything at all.'*

Now behold a miracle, and I know exactly why I'm here—I'm here for the applause. It hits me in full frontal winsomeness, thrilling me to pieces and curling my toes. I love it, I love it. And have to be led, protesting, from the stage.

Miss Kear is my elocution teacher and is so good that already you wouldn't really know I'm native Herefordian. I haven't won my class but I shall have a certificate. And that applause—I'm hooked for ever. Mum is amazed, and Miss Kear—future successes burning in the thick lenses of her spectacles—beams down at me proprietorially. Good old Miss Kear; I love her!

Eleven years old and clandestine at the keyhole I listen to Miss Kear taking Bill through it. He is chairman of the Hereford Licensed Victuallers and tomorrow must make a speech in

tails and sash at the banquet. He has let me hear it: it's funny
and strong and rude and right and I thank God for letting me
be his grandson. But now, on the other side of the lounge door,
Miss Kear is taking him through it, telling him to pause here,
to point there, not to drop his aitches anywhere, rubbing away
all the rough spikiness in return for a bottle of Scotch or gin.
Maybe she'll get two bottles if she manages to smooth most of
him away.

Evelyn Kear is short and chubby, with bright red hair. She
clicks along on high heels which give her the nickname Totty.
When she walks, her legs have the deft, delicate stepping of
pig's trotters, and she runs the Evelyn Kear School of Music,
Elocution and Dramatic Art from her flat over Palamountain's
Wines and Spirits. She bullied Mother into playing the piano
wonderfully well and still has her play for Christmas concerts.
Once Evelyn gets hold she hangs on. She has a special place in
Hereford; she is Miss Showbiz herself.

The Paladium Theatre, Hereford, and out front there's an
expectant buzz as might be expected when the curtain is twenty
minutes late. I am thirteen years old and half an hour away
from my dramatic début as a nineteen-year-old corrupter in
Dodie Smith's *Call It a Day*. It's a Totty Kear production and
we're all in it—Mum, Aunt Thelma and me. Dress rehearsal
ended at one this morning and the grownups are morose and
muttering, though backstage I'm in heaven and watching Totty
trot about as if she were in control. Thelma will let herself go,
forgetting all the direction, and will be a wow; my performance
will be less than memorable and Mother's will be worse—
Evelyn has told her to 'use' her spectacles and she'll put them
on, take them off so many times that she'll have the front four
rows nodding up and down like car-window dogs. A teacher of
mine in the first-night audience will later tell me it's the only
play he's seen where the scene changes not only took longer
than the scenes but were consistently more entertaining.

'Evelyn darling! It was . . . wonderful!'

But now a sense of occasion, if you please. I am fourteen and at a crucial moment. I have dabbled at the piano for years and am desperate for real music at my ambitious fingertips. I am here, above Palamountain's Wines and Spirits, to beseech Miss Kear to bully me into expertise. I can creep through Debussy's '*Clair de lune*' and thump all over Falla's '*Miller's Dance*', but now I want technique, musicianship; I wanna be like my Mummy. I finish the audition and sit expectant as Evelyn silently sums up my prospects and rises to search through her music for something befitting my talent and hopes. She finds the sheet of music and lays it before me; she smiles encouragingly. I'm in! Real music at last.

The music is a popular song for Coronation year. The words go:

> *In a golden coach, there's a heart of gold*
> *That is yearning for you and for me. . . .*

I say no; she says yes. I say no; she says all her other pupils love it. But I say no and her lenses flare briefly: will I be hit by the famous ruler? We compromise—if I will stay with 'Golden Coach' until half-term we'll do something more classical afterwards. But it turns out badly; enthusiasm dies beneath the pure lead of those golden wheels, and I don't even get to half-term.

I'm not popular when I get back to the Commercial and refuse to practise 'Golden Coach'. Trust me to think I know better than Totty . . . or maybe I'm afraid to compete with Mother? Umm, yes; maybe.

Silence please for I am fifteen years old and acting for Miss Kear in her flat above Palamountain's. She sits brooding in the corner of her living room like the saucer-eyed dog in Grimms' fairy tales, casting concentration like some vague, slow-motion net; hit or miss. You can see the thoughts captured: there's the big one—what is she doing with her life here in Hereford? I am concentrating too. Bronze Medal exams for L.A.M.D.A. a few weeks away and the net suddenly swings to me and tightens.

'Why don't you give that character a way of speaking that

is loud—LIKE THIS?' I jump. 'And then soft—like . . .
thisss . . .?'

Why not; I'll try.

'It's what we call onomatopoeia.'

I say no; we've just been doing it in English and onomatopoeia is when a word means what it sounds like, sort of—like
buzz, rattle, clicking.

Totty smiles dangerously. 'It is what we call onomatopoeia.'

I say no, Miss Kear, honest to God it's not. I'll bring the
book if she likes. Roaring of a lion, crashing of a car, mewing
of a kitten; that's onomatopoeia.

She smiles icily. 'That is what we call onomatopoeia.' But
then the chin rises two degrees and the lenses get me square in
their sights and the rough shadow of her alarming reputation
rears over her. I gulp and leave it at that.

I get the Bronze Medal for acting, though not with honours,
which disappoints me. Part of the trouble is Mr. Stickleback's
gestures, in a scene from *Goodbye Mr. Chips*. I invent a throw-
away gesture with old Mr. Stickleback's left hand and Evelyn
is enraptured; she makes me do it again and again; I have to
show other pupils, her friends. By the time we come to the
exam I have built the gesture so much that the scene becomes
a three-hander between old Mr. Stickleback, young Mr. Chips
and old Mr. Stickleback's left arm and the examiner doesn't
seem so enraptured as Totty.

Dead silence please for here I am at sixteen, stepping up to the
stage in the Percival Hall for my Silver Medal exam. I'm
desperate for honours this time and I've rehearsed my scenes
and monologue beyond all call of duty. I'm fresh from my
success as the porter in a school *Macbeth* and nothing's going
to stop me now. There's a dim pool of light on stage and far
out in the hall I can see the examiner's shaded lamp. Silence.
This is it.

I step forward and announce myself; he tells me to begin.
It's the toughest test so far: two scenes, and all characters are
female; the monologue's from *Saint Joan*. Totty Kear is de-

lighted with my work. I launch confidently into a scene adapted from Jane Austen and have been hard at it for maybe half a minute when I'm aware of stirring from the auditorium.

'Excuse me.'

I stop. What's wrong?

'I'm afraid there's been some mistake. Do you know you're doing the section for girls only?' He laughs. I begin to crumble. 'I think there's been a slight slip-up. Miss Kear?'

He looks round for Evelyn. So do I. 'Miss Kear?'

In my red-faced fury I hear Totty click towards the dim glow near the back of the hall. Murmurs drift to me. The examiner speaks. 'Let's go on, shall we?'

So we do. What else is there to do? But it's dreadful. My carefully observed and constructed feminine voice and movement are grotesque now that I know it's all a terrible mistake. I dry up twice. Christ, I'm a drag queen out of drag; I must look a real sissy and my ears are honed to catch the slightest giggle from waiting candidates in the wings—God help the first titterer as I blunder on, missing honours by a mile. It's my last appearance definitely on any stage . . . well maybe. It's certainly the last for Totty Kear.

A year or so later Evelyn was run down by a bus in Cardiff. Stepping daintily from a pavement even those huge lenses failed to see it bearing down on her and she died outright.

Hereford was shocked and I did my best to feel sorry for her death.

Instead I thought of Miss Kear's butterfly mind fluttering round Bill's genuine banquet speech, nibbling it down to her own level. I thought of the loss of my rich Herefordian voice. I thought of 'How sad a thing' and 'Golden Coach' whose desperate triviality comes clearly through the years. I remembered *Call It a Day*, Mr. Stickleback's left arm, onomatopoeia and the embarrassment in the Percival Hall. Suddenly the nightmare vision hit me of an army of Evelyn Kears, golden and fêted in every provincial city, casting a grotesque shadow of glamour on an even greater army of stage-struck, dance-bedevilled, elocution-hungry, piano-charmed boys and girls who would, in turn, send *their* children to other Miss Kears. I saw a vista of gala performances in Town Halls, Christmas concerts, charity matinées; children in bedrooms rehearsing L.A.M.D.A. scenes, playing all the characters, schizophrenically turning this way and that, talking with voices, inventing gestures.

And suddenly, yes, I was very sorry indeed about poor Totty. What the outrageous hosts of Miss Kears may have spread over the children of earlier decades may not actually have been culture but it was different and, yes, it was fun—fun in a time of drabness, poverty and depression. We badly needed Evelyn Kears and I mourned, in a fashion, one who'd had style and got away with it for years. I would hate Miss Kear to teach any kid of mine, but the warm and genuine laughter that her prancing birdlike figure and over-elocutionized quacking provokes—and how she would have hated it, mistaking it merely for mocking—testifies how much I owe her, would not have missed her for anything.

꧖ Jimmy Lewis

I used to spend much time gazing down upon Commercial Road from my bedroom at the top of the pub, watching the changing scene—the comings and goings at the bus station opposite, and, at nights, the patient queuing outside the Ritz: the road was almost always interesting. For many years, one of the sights that both amused and worried me was the flat-footed figure of Ikey in his long torn coat shuffling God knows where and constantly tormented by whatever small boys happened to be available for the purpose. Always his steps would be dogged by these shrill tormentors whose falsetto insults seldom rose the three storeys to my window—though his furious obscenities nearly always did.

If ever I crossed his path, I was humble, smiling. If I was lucky, I would receive no more than a flurry of suspicious glances and mutterings; unlucky, I would be screamed at and waved away at high speed. I never knew what happened to Ikey or where his endless ramblings along Commercial Road took him. Ikey was truly crazed and I was not of an age to wonder with what inner life he believed himself involved.

Another sad figure was the legless beggar slumped, cap on pavement, against the wall of the wool and skin factory, whom I once rashly invited to my birthday party, though I do not remember him coming and think I would if he had turned up. My compassion for this man turned me into a virtual beggar myself: I think he was eventually moved on, probably with a substantial donation, by Bill who soon tired of my endless demands for small coins to throw into the cap.

Jimmy Lewis, though simple, was like neither of these unfortunates, though, in less sympathetic circumstances, he might
have ended up like one or the other. For a start, he had a brother
who kept an eye on him—a large, unsmiling man who had a
small shop near the other end of the road, a magic place to a
child, selling everything from sweets and sherbet, out of jars,
to shoe polish and writing paper. Another big difference was
that Jimmy was part of the pub; he belonged with us. He was
Public Bar trade. He was a mild, happy soul with a slack,
smiling mouth and a disconcerting walk which most closely
resembled a lope. Watching him as he moved along the road,
from high above, I decided there was no coordination between
his striding legs and his stiff arms. I seldom remember him
troubled, though when a bitter mood was upon him his stride
would increase and his mouth move into a hard muttering line.

He had many friends in the pub and enjoyed both the company and the fun; a drink or three would make him a beaming
lighthouse of *bonhomie* and the cheapness of cider, coupled with
his likeability, kept him well supplied. Between the extremes
of his moods there was a characteristic puzzlement: Jim was the
only man I ever saw, outside novels and films, to push back his
cap and scratch his head in bewilderment. His simple nature
made him an obvious target for jokes and he was often sent on
pointless errands. But Jimmy enjoyed the jokes as much as the
perpetrators, whether he understood them or not, and this drew
the sting from the cruelty, and often turned the joke back upon
its originators. I liked Jimmy. The lack of spite or resentment
set him apart from malcontents like Ikey and his sense of fun,
and the fact that he was—though sometimes only just—em-
ployable, gave him a greater acceptability than the beggar
near the front door steps. He was always respectful to my grandparents, who responded with occasional generosity and even
less occasional employment. When the clamour of his laughter
rang loudly through the pub, even the customers in the Private
Bar would grin at each other and say 'Eyup; he's away!'

Jimmy was capable of surprises. He professed enjoyment of
football and turned up one day with a tray of flags and collecting

tin, gathering cash for refugees of some sort. To our astonished questioning, he replied that his efforts were all for Hereford United, and it was some little time before we realized he had confused the officials for the Saturday matches with the displaced unfortunates he was collecting for. Refugees, not referees. I don't recall anyone putting him straight and we all piled coins into his tin and sent him up the road to the Great Western where they would enjoy the joke too.

Occasionally he appeared encased in placards, a sandwich man, advertising whatever had to be advertised, and it was in this guise that he gave me my most enjoyable and vivid memory of him. Jimmy was an obsessive collector of second-hand tobacco; any half-smoked, unsmoked dog-end was grabbed from the pavement or even gutter and snapped into a tin to be later reconstituted into ill-shaped and evil-smelling smokes. As he loped along, his eyes swept the concrete before him like out-of-water Asdic, seeking out any likely contribution. Wearing placards, of course, restricted this activity, and one day in Commercial Road, I saw him bend instinctively for a fat cigarette butt and almost knock himself unconscious as his swiftly descending chin struck the top edge of the boards. But Jimmy was not to be deterred; he tried again, gently, but still, as he crouched and groped for his prize, the boards rose to obstruct his view and force his chin almost vertical. He tried it sideways, eyes swivelling down, but his balance was precarious and he had to stand again. Eventually, he stepped back and, looking down towards the Commercial, about a hundred yards away, he set off with great delicacy towards assistance, moving the offending stub with his foot, prodding it along at the end of his toe cap. I will never know why he didn't simply remove the boards, collect his booty and carry on towards High Town, or how he managed to judge where exactly the mess of tobacco, growing more shapeless as he progressed, lay beneath the skirts of wood. He slowly drew nearer until, with about half the distance covered, he stopped and drew back, and he and the tobacco glared at each other. This silent communion stretched into long seconds, and then, swamped by defeat, he lifted a foot and scrubbed the cigarette end into annihilation before setting off purposefully the way he had come. If the dog-end were not to be his, he was sure it wasn't going to be anyone else's.

He was an occasional surprise to me, and to anyone from a more sheltered background whom I was trying to impress, in later years, when he would greet me with noisy affection around the town. But I never lost a girl friend this way—the account of the placard incident was always a bonus to the evening. And I hope he is still about. He was eventually taken into some sort of care and when I saw him, several months ago, he looked older, his craggy face so dry and pale it almost seemed as if he were powdered. But the lope was still purposeful, though trousered in a smart suit, and he held a mackintosh over one arm. He did not recognize me and I thought some spark had left him. I hoped somebody had not screwed his cheerful anarchy out of existence beneath an official boot, as he had ruined his offending tobacco all those years before in Commercial Road one Saturday morning when we were both younger.

೪ The Real Thing

A SENTIMENTAL ROMANCE IN THE OLD STYLE

I was the last one it should have happened to. Me, the pub kid, close neighbour to the skin factory and slaughterhouse, caught up in the very un-romantic world of booze, dirty jokes, smutty songs. Me, the daybug at my school who had fumbled un-romantically with Margery and Ann in the desperate attempt to find out what the dirt was all about, with half the ceiling and one complete wall of my bedroom lewd with pin-ups. I was not the type. It is altogether impossible that at Kimnel Park, near Rhyl, in two hot summer weeks not long before my eighteenth birthday, I should have fallen for the first and only time, with an intensity that frightens me even now, headlong into a love so deep, so frantic and, above all, so pure that the fortnight, and the year, that followed it seem now to belong to someone entirely different, an alien maybe from outer space, and that the wonder who brought all this about should not only be three years younger but that *his* name should be Mike.

In retrospect it is not so surprising. It has taken me years to realize, to my growing astonishment, that in that crowded pub, a centre of attention, I was a lonely as well as an only child. When I consider the wholehearted fervour with which I plunged into life at school, into my Scout troop, into the holidays at Stone Farm with Betty Barwell's band of brothers and adoptees, I see I was desperate for acceptance and commitment —I suppose, simply, for love. When I lost my heart at Kimnel I was ready for someone in particular to find it and am still glad it was Mike.

The School cadet force was at camp and I was its senior cadet, the company sergeant-major. These camps came nearest my vague fantasies of being a boarder in a public school, a sort of warm and sticky distillation of Greyfriars, Tom Brown's Rugby and every other private school that lower-middle-class boys used to find so fascinating in comics and novels. It was July, and in August I would return to school as captain, leading also the Fifteen, playing Faustus in the Dramatic Society production. I mention all this small beer because it was important then: I was bettering myself, getting on, fulfilling the blueprints that had been laid down for me. It was a dangerous time, merging fantasy and reality, where wish fulfilment actually happened and I was wonderfully happy.

The camp at Kimnel Park was identical to the four other camps I'd attended. On a bleak plain a small township of brown canvas had been set up; radio aerials were everywhere; four-ton Army trucks destroyed grass in great quantities: the Army had made its usual mess of nature in order to encourage the recruitment and training of T.A. and C.C.F. forces from all over the country. With us at Kimnel were about twenty C.C.F. contingents from public schools of greater and lesser fame. We always believed that our accents and general lack of polish singled us out, but this was merely a symptom, self-inflicted, of insecurity among bigger and worldlier folk than us. We ran through a parody of Army life more or less with enjoyment. I was an easygoing C.S.M., arrogant only when necessary. It was the pub all over again: putting on the style, swopping faces behind the one mask.

Mike was a boarder whose parents had separated. He lived mostly with his mother in South Norwood but was proud of his father, a captain in the regular Army with whom he stayed at the week-end once or twice a term. Like me, Mike was not particularly attractive or sensuous, and sex never came twisting into the pure Eden of our romance: we agreed it would ruin the relationship anyway—we saw enough of that at school. The rest of our company took our mutual devotion entirely for granted and we were soon accepted as inseparable: my good friend, Dangle, who was in charge of the field telephones, actually added Mike's name below mine on the card over the telephone exchange in the company office where our masters/ officers must have seen it, and even they took no notice, not one sarcastic reference.

Strangely—or perhaps, in a romance like ours, typically— I had never spoken to Mike in the two years he had been at the school, but, one enchanted evening when a number of us were passing time together, he came to the fringe of the group. Buster was chafing Andrew about how he'd managed to wangle a place in the same tent as Drop whom he liked, and I made some mock self-pitying remark on the sadness of having a tent all to myself. There was dutiful, friendly laughter, all of them knowing that the exclusive tent was a much-prized perk of the job and highly valued, in particular by me, as a badge of office, when Mike said, 'I'd better come in with you, then,' surprising everyone because he was not at all the pushing type, hardly knew me, was content in the School House bloc, was risking a heavy put-down. There was more laughter and some badinage which he weathered easily.

'It's crowded in our tent anyway.' He looked at me solemnly, for the first time. 'Okay?'

And breezily I said sure, okay, fine, and moved the subject hastily on to the gunnery demonstration we were to see to-morrow. In fact, I was knocked flat, for once caught for an answer, babbling senselessly of twenty-five pounders without hearing a word I was saying. I had encountered something entirely new: someone was choosing *me* for a change. I would not have chosen Mike, of all people, even considered him, but he had chosen me and that was something, though what I didn't know.

He tactfully waited until no one was about, including me, to transfer his blankets and straw mattress into the C.S.M.'s tent, and when I next came there, his bedding was laid out and he was seated in the doorway, polishing my boots. From then on it was roses, roses all the way. That night we lay on our separate beds, holding hands and listening to Gershwin's

'Rhapsody in Blue', played on the harmonica by Larry Adler, courtesy of Radio Israel via another perk, a 33 radio with extra headphones. When it had finished, I said, 'I think you're terrific, Mike.' Mike said, 'I like you a lot.' And we went to sleep. Violins! Choir! Strew the page with violets! Why is it we remember so disastrously verbatim the B feature dialogue of our lives!

But I was vibrant as the rest of the camp passed in talking together, walking together, eating and swimming together and in anticipation of being together when we weren't. I was on air, at entire peace, feeling a new completeness, and Mike felt the same. The emotion doubled back from one to the other, compounding itself and making of us new and different people from the two kids we had been a week or so earlier.

I remember our parting as one of the more miserable times of my life: I had no similar experiences to set philosophically against it and it tore me. The night before we had spent mostly in silence; we swapped watches—something tangible that had been close to the other person—and in the morning we watched each other sombrely out of sight, Mike in the back of a truck bound for the London train. On the long journey to Hereford I sat in deep melancholy, impressing those who knew the reason —and I probably made sure they did: an exhibitionist in love is still an exhibitionist.

At the Kite's Nest I grieved. I had always felt a sort of blankness when I left Stone Farm, the Scout camps, other C.C.F. camps, but this was yet another new feeling: it was sharp and did not diminish within the customary day or two. My parents must have been aware that something was wrong. They noticed the watch and I had to invent a fatuous story. We wrote letters, of course, at once, but resisted the pressure to phone more than once a week, twice at most, for another element had crept into our awareness. We were no longer in the safety of Kimnel's private world and there was simply no way we could even begin to explain our mutual devotion to the families we found ourselves having to live with as if nothing had happened. I suppose that if either of us had had more money or more spirit we would probably have not stayed apart but we were both complaisant and poor. As the sending and receiving of letters increased our passion for each other we began to make plans for Mike to spend a few days at the Kite immediately before the new term, and began casually sowing the seeds of the idea in our respective homes, dismally aware of the intervening six weeks.

That summer, the sense of loss never weakened, and eventually I had to speak to somebody about it. I confided in my two best friends. Sid was his usual ironic self and noncommittal but could see I was genuinely disturbed and not to be mocked. Percy, on the other hand, seemed merely distant; I wondered if I'd shocked him and was astounded and relieved to have a long letter by the next available post telling me he understood perfectly, and sympathized, for he was in a similar position. His confession made me feel good, proving that such a relationship could work and remain concealed. And the holidays stretched ahead.

In August, Mike moved north to join his father at Catterick and I moved south to attend a cadet course with 42 Commando at Plymouth, intrigued by the heroic nature of it. Communications had been arranged with suitably military precision: he sent me, as soon as he could, the number of a phone box near the camp and I phoned him there each night at nine. I was grateful for the chance to speak to him privately, without fear of lurking adults, and also because our nightly conversations— absurdly, in retrospect—established a sense of reality which my weeks with the Commando were beginning to destroy. After a day spent learning to kill my fellow men (particularly, on one day, with my bare hands: 'But remember, lads: you must never put into action what you've practised here today.' 'No sir'), it was good to hear someone I loved and to chat about nothing in particular. The course came to an end—the only casualty, deliciously, a Commando sergeant who had broken his leg showing off to us—and I went home to Hereford with about three weeks' holiday left.

With Mike's visit now a matter of days away I began to have severe apprehensions: if my feelings had let me, I would have called it off—after all, we would be with each other at school very soon. For the first time, I really began to imagine what my parents would make of him, and the fact, which I knew would be impossible to hide, that we were very close. Our respective mothers had exchanged letters which paved the way pleasantly, but Mike's had made some reference to the fact that we seemed very good friends despite the slight age gap, and when Mother wanted to know the extent of the gap I lied, telling her he was almost sixteen; in South Norwood, as it turned out, Mike had lied that I was just seventeen. In fact, he was just fifteen, and I almost eighteen. Our letters and phone calls increased in devotion and slowly the days were ticked off in my diary. Five days before the new term, six weeks after my last sight of him, two months since falling in love, Mike and I came face to face at Hereford station and at that instant I knew it could not work out.

From that moment on, I let Mike down almost constantly. I had never seen him in any clothes but his cadet outfits and school uniform; in singlet and slacks he looked young—too young. And I was known by people on the platform. He came hurrying happily towards me as I stood guiltily near the exit. For one tricky moment I thought he was going to hug me but instead we stood there, grinning, and then we walked from the station to catch a bus home. Neither seemed to say anything, after the initial greetings. In fact it was difficult to know exactly what could be said, for the always-increasing fervour of our letters and calls had swept us to such a lofty viewpoint that ordinary day-to-day conversation seemed a little silly. I wondered how his thoughts were running. He seemed the same Mike that I had loved at Kimnel, but this was not Kimnel and I wondered if that one irremovable fact, petty by comparison with our feelings, might not destroy us. Side by side, waiting for the bus, I became definitely aware that it really mattered to me what my mother would think, what Les, what Nan, what my friends would think about bringing a boy friend back to Hereford. I began to let Mike down.

Mother made him welcome enough and Les was polite and

shy. The few days passed without too many difficulties, and why not, since they were entirely of my own imagining. Mike's room was at one end of the building and mine at the other. When that first night, I went in to say good-night, he reached up to me. 'Come here, you!' and hugged me.

I said blankly, 'Good-night, Mike,' and disengaged myself at once, to go back to my room.

Next morning, early, I heard his door close and his steps pad along the landing and he came happily in, ruffled my hair and plonked down on the bed, Kimnel Mike. But one thin wall away, my parents would be awake, too—they may even have heard the plonk. I winced at the idea of their listening; silence would probably worry them more than noise, but what to say? Mike said quietly, 'How are you then?' and slid an arm behind my head—and then I was suddenly out of bed and dressing, chatting loudly. Mike smiled, but did not come early to see me again.

Only once was there any comment about the unsuitability of Mike as a friend. One morning he got up specially early and took the cat to play on the lawn in the crisp sun. He had on his singlet and an absurd pair of children's shorts that made him look about twelve. He teased the cat, shouting, 'Pussycar! Pussycar!' From an upstairs window Mother and I watched the pair of them frolicking, and she said, reproachfully, 'He's very young.'

I was relieved when term began; it would be better for us there. Nearer Kimnel. I told Mike I was sorry the Kite's Nest had not been a success and that school would be better. He smiled and said he'd enjoyed the stay. Boarders had to return one day early, and we had lunch in a café in Hereford before going into the school in mid-afternoon. There were several others about; we gazed at the notice on the board confirming my appointment of captain of the school. Mike was very proud of me. He kept pointing at the notice, saying, 'That's you! That's you!'

So Mike went back to School House and I moved to the Commercial, in Hereford—autumn term was very busy for me, with rugby practice each day after school and *Faustus* rehearsals most nights: it was easier for me to live there, with Nan, and company for her. But for Mike and me, school was not the success I'd fervently hoped for. Our daily, weekly patterns were simply not compatible. Except for the week-ends, the only free time Mike as a boarder ever had was the two-hour gap between afternoon school and tea, and that was the time I trained for rugby; after that, he was locked up in School House. At week-ends I had to go to the Kite's Nest after the match, and I did not want him there again—anyway, it would have meant him getting his mother's permission each time. I used to see him often, but never alone except when impossible conditions cancelled the Fifteen's training schedule; then he would borrow a cycle and drive through the rain to share tea with me in the kitchen of the Commercial and our relationship, which had become so complicated, simplified in the pleasure of each other's exclusive company. In spite of these occasional moments, imperceptibly and unwillingly we began to cool down. One day, while Nan and I were getting a bar straight for opening, she said, 'How's your little boy?' which was fine, but then, confused, added, 'Oh, I shouldn't say that, should I?' which rang clear bells that the family had been chewing it all over and didn't know what to make of it but had their suspicions.

I went on letting Mike down. I let him down publicly in the day boy monitors' common room where he had formed the habit of visiting me during break and occasionally after lunch. Some of my fellow monitors had been at Kimnel. Buster and Dangle, for instance, were content to have Mike a frequent visitor; Sid and Percy too. Others were more possessive about the M.C.R. and I was quietly asked to cut down on his appearances. I couldn't bring myself to do this and eventually he was shown the door firmly after having been particularly hearty and boring, while I sat on the radiators reading a book, pretending it was a sort of joke. After being ushered out on other occasions, less and less politely, he stopped calling altogether, unless he knew I was alone, or with friends who accepted him. Weirdly, I kidded myself *he* was letting *me* down; it was easier that way.

Mike spent Christmas split between South Norwood and Catterick. Our letters surprised us by kindling something of the fierce affection we seemed to have lost; perhaps it would be more honest to say that Mike had always written like that: it was shaming to find that he was the constant star and I the wavering lover. But in a sense, our bluff—*my* bluff—had been called at school. The hopes, fears, protestations that filled the pages had to be set against the general disapproval of the M.C.R. and the fact that we seldom met.

Spring term was another busy time for us both: he had O levels, and I had A levels. For me there was yet more rugby and yet another play, acting for the Hereford Players, an amateur group, fun to be with; but we met when we could, though I'm sure that even Mike must have had the feeling we were running down in neutral. Yet he never reproached me. Perhaps it was this realization that prompted him to make a plan to take us away at half-term, and over which I let him down hard and cruelly.

The plan was that we should travel for half-term to his father who had already agreed to fiddle travel warrants for us if we travelled in cadet uniform. It was a good idea to search for another Kimnel and I gave it little thought at the beginning of term, let him get on with the arrangements. But I should have checked dates. The final performance of my amateur play was timed for the British Drama League festival in Hereford and fell on the second night of half-term; by the time adjudication had been given and the results announced it would be well past eleven, too late to set out for Catterick. Either Mike or the Players would have to go. Mike was generous in his understanding of this and rearranged his plans: he would travel up on Friday night, as arranged, and I would follow on Sunday morning, which still gave us about a day and a half. If I preferred, he would wait to travel with me, though it would mean finding someone to put him up for two nights.

At the last minute I chickened out of the whole arrangement from sheer cowardice, using feeble excuses of tiredness, A level work, etc. The imminence of the week-end had set up apprehensions similar to those I had felt as Mike's stay at the Kite had come closer. All other people's fathers held a powerful mystique for me, and when meeting Mike's became a near reality, guilt came knocking again at my resolution—the only spare room had just the one double bed, for God's sake. What would he think of that? Mike had willingly faced Mother and Les, but I was less brave and cancelled my part in the visit only two days before the school packed up for the brief holiday.

It was a rotten thing to do. His father wanted to meet me and give me a good time to thank me for being kind to Mike. Mike wanted to show me off—I was a senior under-officer now —and spend time alone with me. I wanted a week-end with Mike, to try to claw our way back to the happy simplicity of Kimnel. But my guilts—with nothing to be guilty about—had grown sturdily throughout the six months and were blooming cripplingly well now. The thought of the Captain and the double bed were genuinely alarming, for no reason beyond myself, but because I saw myself in his place, as I had seen myself in my parents' room listening to silence. Transferring my own fears to everyone else in sight, I worried myself into inertia, and not only let Mike down but even managed to blame him for some of it, which is real high-class hypocrisy, and at only eighteen.

I had cried plenty about Mike but this was the only time I ever saw him come near tears. He said nothing as I made my feeble excuses, but his eyes filled. There was an awkward pause. He had to speak quietly, for Ian Johnson was in the common room.

'Don't you *want* to come?' I had no answer. 'It's all fixed.'

The silence lengthened, and then Ian, who was also in the play and knew something but not much about what was happening, quickly got up. 'Come on.' It was an authoritarian command. He threw my coat to me. Ian did not like Mike.

I dithered.

'There's only an hour to go.' Another command, offering me a way out.

Before I could take it, Mike had left. He had a good half-term, he told me. He never reproached me.

Easter holidays came and went. We occasionally wrote dutiful letters. I phoned South Norwood once and thought Mike's mother was off-hand and cool, so I phoned no more. A level work grew heavy and I stopped writing.

It was a shock to recall, that summer term, that Kimnel Park was almost a year in the past. Mike and I were very much involved in exams and we saw little of each other until they were over. It was yet another shock when he told me he was leaving at the end of the school year for Welbeck and a military career and would not be coming to the annual camp at Folkstone because there was too much to get ready. When I asked him if our relationship had anything to do with either decision he smiled and told me not to be silly.

Under pressure of this news I made a final bid to salvage something, too young to know that any extreme experience moves at once beyond recapture. I set about arranging a special adventure camp in the Black Mountains on the borders of England and Wales. Tony, a fellow under-officer in the C.C.F., destined for Sandhurst, and I had often knocked the idea about, and I set to putting our vague ideas into immediate action. We took them to the Major and he was enthusiastic, letting me work out all details and arrange all training; I was to order the equipment from the Army at Brecon who would deliver it to the site which he, Tony and I chose from the ordnance survey map. The adventure camp was arranged for August and Tony and I hand-picked about a dozen cadets who would enjoy an adventurous week and be competent enough to make a success of it. Mike was the first one I asked; he agreed, asking to be in charge of first aid. If Mike had not been so entirely honest and genuine I might have considered it a careful revenge when he withdrew from the scheme a week before the end of term: there was simply no time, he said. I felt grey, landed with the bloody Black Mountain adventure for nothing: Mike and the fading vision of a second Kimnel had been more than half the motivation.

On the last full day of Mike's time in Hereford, on the last day of my last summer term, Mike and I drove on my newly-acquired motor bike to Dinmore Woods. We found a lonely high point commanding a splendid view and sat in silence, holding embarrassed hands. The year had spun the web between us and there was no hope of explaining it away. Kimnel had gone. My susceptibilities for my public image, and my cowardice, had anaesthetized everything between us. It wasn't that either of us had another relationship, even.

So the sun went splendidly down towards Radnorshire and we watched it, closed in separate feelings, with nothing worth saying. At last we got up and dusted ourselves down before driving back to Hereford in time for boarders' tea. I have no memories of parting, next day.

And that was the big, the only pure romance of my life; no relationship since has ever had the impact, for which I've come to be grateful. I learned from it that being in love and loving someone are not at all the same. It was pure public school, too; a standard part of every school novel from *Tom Brown* on.

Malcolm Muggeridge has expressed gratitude that his own school was wretched and unlovable since it has left no rose-tinted claims on him as others among his contemporaries seem to have felt from their school days—and I went back to my school, some six years later, as a tutor, which seems to prove his point. Lord Rosebery, on the other hand, dying in 1929, asked that the Eton Boating Song should be the final sound of his life. I count myself as free an agent as most men and yet the horrific truth is that sometimes, as now, at the end of my sentimental romance, I feel that Rosebery was right, too. There but for the Grace of God . . .

So if you'll just move over, my Lord, and happen to have a recording of Larry Adler playing the 'Rhapsody in Blue' . . .